Numerology Workbook using Chaldean Mysticism

Andras M. Nagy

ISBN: 978-1-968194-20-8

Table of Contents

Preface

This book is a workbook to teach you the basic calculations of a Numerology chart using the Chaldean system[1]. Most books written on Numerology are using the Western, also known as the Pythagorean system. It also must be said that too many numerology books are assuming computers or phone apps that will leave us ignorant when the battery on the Mobile phone is low or the computer is broken. Numerology calculations are very simple and the only tools you'd need is paper and pencil.

Is Numerology a Divination or Personality Analysis? Many people use numerology as a divination tool but a precious few are good at it[2]. I consider it more of a personality, character analysis then fortune telling. I behold self knowledge as an immense value and using Numerology to analyzing a child's potential can be a great asset. Lastly, I favor using Numerology to determine if I would embark on important venues on certain auspicious days or not.

Seeing certain numbers or number patters could be a celestial or otherworldly warning so I pay attention to numbers on my odometer or other odd places through out my daily life.

The Chaldean System is older than the Pythagorean system and it is based on the numbers 1 through 8, not 1 through 9. The Chaldean system incorporates Astrology into the analysis, which to me, made this older system even more appealing.

Pythagoras himself may have been exposed to Eastern mystery schools as he traveled in Egypt and Babylonia while in exile.

The Chaldean system also uses colors[3] and gemology to enforce the effectiveness of our numbers. As the causal effect of numbers , planetary movements, colors, music etc is

---

[1] Closer to the Vedic Numerology this system uses a different table for name analysis.

[2] Cheiro was the few who was excellent but his exact methods and system remained a secret. He used Astrology and Palmistry along with Numerology to make The Chaldean System is older than the Pythagorean system and it is based on the numbers 1 through 8, not 1 through 9. The Chaldean system incorporates Astrology into the analysis, making uncanny predictions.

[3] the Law of Colors : All colors are centers of attraction, and are complementary or are antipathetic to each other. Color is healing and impacts the physical, emotional, mental and human body profoundly. Man is partially composed of color in the aura (we are color, tone, symbols and speed of vibration, or light). When intense rays of one or more colors are sent to a specific area of the body, change results.

vibration we should pay close attention to our surroundings. My former Yoga teacher's Guru RHH was a well-known interior designer. He had an uncanny talent of mixing colors to paint walls that were magical for the ambiance of the room. The room all of the sudden was imbued with a certain healing quality. That's what colors can do for you.

Red	1
Orange	2
Yellow	3
Green	4
Blue	5
Purple	6
Black	7
Gray	8
White	9

A great part of the two systems are overlapping since they are the same when considering the numbers and cycles derived from the date of birth. The difference comes in when we calculate numbers from the name(s) we use different tables. The Chaldean is often referred as a phonetic system because the letters and number assigned using more of a phonetic scheme.

Until the past year, I have been using and promoting the Pythagorean systems, especially the software written by Hans Decoz. Recently, I have realized the need for a workbook like this, to teach and promote Chaldean Numerology and Astrology as a viable tools for self-discovery and self-help.

The Philosophy of Numbers goes back to the Ancient times when religion and philosophy were interchangeable and men observed nature. In Romeo and Juliet, Shakespeare, the closet mystic and creative and philosophical genius posed the question; "*A rose by any other name would smell as sweet*"?" Questioning the weight a name carries in the context of the underlying attributes of the subject.

All these are part of what I call magical thinking, a world view and philosophy that presupposes that we live in an orderly Universe where most things are choreographed to perfection. Indeed, when we closely observe nature at the level of the macrocosm or the microcosm[4] things turn to be amazingly orderly and even similar; hence the old Hermetic saying; "as above, so is below".

The terminology of Numerology books are rather confusing. Since the Decoz software is widely known, I will use the Decoz naming of various numbers in this workbook. Concurring with the Chaldean philosophy of numbers, master numbers as such are not used in this text.

It must be mentioned I have heavily used material, now in the public domain and written by the Master Cherio and to honor his memory, please read the following chapter on his life and accomplishments.

---

[4] Atomic and sub atomic structures resemble the stars.

The Basics

Numerology draws its conclusions from your birth-date and name. There are core numbers and auxiliary numbers. A good numerology system is three faceted. a) it uses the appropriate methods of calculations, b) it uses the correct letter -to-number conversion scheme, and finally c) it has the appropriate description of the numbers at any given stage.

Numerology works because throughout the years intuitive people after analyzing numerous cases, had noticed patterns of human behavior and talents used or wasted in well-known people. Numerology (or Astrology) would not work on the Buddha, as he had transcended the typical follies of human existence. It however works on average people who are caught in the revolving door of life/death and reincarnation. Numerology can assist you in selecting a proper career, a proper name for your child, analyzing your mate and friends for more intimate knowledge. Knowing the past intimately would allow us to peek into the future and guide us not to repeat the same mistakes.

The Numbers deriving from the birth-date are:
- Life Path (core number)
- Birth-day (auxiliary number)
- Challenges (auxiliary numbers of various stages of life)
- Pinnacle (auxiliary numbers of various stages of life)

The Numbers deriving from the name are:
- Expression (core number)
- Heart's Desire (core number, derived from the Vowels of the name)
- Personality(core number, derived from the Consonants of the name)
- Karmic Debt(auxiliary number)

The Maturity Number (core number) comprises of by adding the Life Path and Expression Numbers together. Each number listed has a chapter dedicated where examples and interpretation is given.

To double check our calculation we should add The Heart's Desire and Personality digits, which should be the same as the Expression digit. If for some reason we have two differing number then somehow our calculation has an error.

Who was Cheiro?

William John Warner, known as Cheiro, (November 1, 1866 —October 8, 1936) was an Irish astrologer and colorful occult figure of the early 20th century. His pen-name, Cheiro, derives from the word chiromancy, meaning palmistry. He was a documented clairvoyant who taught palmistry, astrology, and Chaldean numerology. During his career, he was celebrated for using these forms of divination to make personal predictions for famous clients and to foresee world events. In his memoirs it was described that as a teenager, he traveled to the Bombay port of Apollo Bunder. There, he met his Guru, an Indian Brahmin, who took him to his village in the valley of the Konkan region of Maharashtra. Later Cheiro was permitted by Brahmans to study an ancient book that has many studies on hands; the pages of the book were made of human skin and written with gold and it is still guarded and protected with great care. After studying thoroughly for two years, he returned to London and started his career as a palmist.

At the peak of his career Cheiro had a wide following of famous European and American clients during the late 19th and early 20th centuries. He read palms and told the fortunes of famous celebrities like Mark Twain, W. T. Stead, Sarah Bernhardt, Mata Hari, Oscar Wilde, Grover Cleveland, Thomas Edison, the Prince of Wales, General Kitchener, William Ewart Gladstone, and Joseph Chamberlain. He documented his sittings with these clients by asking them to sign a guest book he kept for the purpose, in which he encouraged them to comment on their experiences as subjects of his character analyses and predictions. Of the Prince of Wales, he wrote that "I would not be surprised if he did not give up everything, including his right to be crowned, for the woman he loved." Cheiro also predicted that the Jews would return to Palestine and the country would again be called Israel.

After some years in London, and many world travels, Cheiro moved to America. He spent his final years in Hollywood, seeing as many as twenty clients a day and doing some screenwriting before his death there in 1936 following a heart attack. His widow, the Countess Lena Hamon, said her 70-year-old husband, who had been a friend and adviser to film actors late in life, and to European aristocracy and royalty in his early career, had predicted his own death to the hour the day.

As very prolific and talented writer, he wrote several books mainly focusing on soothsaying and occult matters. In his autobiography Cherio was very frank admitting that he never quite understood his unique "gift" and that he had lost his foresight in 1906, as a result of a personal failure and a brief prison sentence for mishandling certain funds of a client. He never regained his fame and fortune and died rather poor.

Part I. Using the Birth Date

The Life-Path

This number is calculated using our birth date hence also called a "fadic" number. Some numerologist also use the terminology as a Destiny Number or Birth Force Number[5]. The dates of your birth are cycles in the Universe, based on the planetary forces there is an exact three ringed cycle the Month the Day and the Year of your birth. When the planets were aligned precisely like thus, it was an important date for your parents and relatives, not to mention you, as a person. You came to be as a individual, with your whole life ahead of you, ready for the journey. This number will reveal to you what your general path might look like. This path is not carved into stone rather it is drawn in sand, leaving you leeway for your attitude and choices you will have to make along the way[6]. Also, it is very important to understand - your outlook of life - positive or negative thinking can influence the outcome what this number potentially represent.

Because we are dealing with three different planetary cycles, these dates are to be calculated separately and the sum finally totaled.

Month   1-12 (January =1, February=2 etc)
Day   1-31
Year   four digits

The digital root

Numerology always ignores the quantity the number would represent, usually (but not always) it looks at the digital root of any two or more digits by adding up the digits you will get the digital root. For example;

27 is 2+7= 9
36 is 3+6=9

Also, in this case 27 or 72 are the same 9's but the 27 has the 2 which is the first one, called the cornerstone number making it distinctly different.

The other way to look at this that the series of numbers, like 27. The digits represent a different shade of a color of the same composition. A 9 derived from a 27 has some trace elements of a 2 as well as some archetypical elements of a 7, but ultimately it is a 9. When you mix colors you use blue and yellow, thus getting a similar shade but not the same.

---

[5] I have seen books using the name *Life Lesson*, hinting that this is a key why we a reincarnated i.e. the main lesson to learn/correct but I do not think this is so.
[6] Even thou the result maybe the same this is a good practice to learn to acquire the proper thinking and spirit of this art.

My favorite Beatle, George Harold Harrison was born in Liverpool on 25 February 1943. Lets look at George Harrison's Life Path Number.

Month 2 (February) = 2
Day 25 - 2+5=7
Year 1943 - 1+9+4+3 =8
Total the 3 lines - 2+7+8=8

Clearly, the number 8 is a perfect interpretation for a hard working and ambitious person on a not very easy path. The 8 is not easy path because it is a combination of the higher and lower spheres. It becomes crystal clear if you just look at the symbolism of the snowman like 8, the upper circle represents the higher realms and the lower, bigger (fatter) circle the lower realms. Waking this path is nothing of a cakewalk, rather it is akin to walking the razor's edge. No wonder that George Harrison tried drugs and other excesses that were clearly available to these superstars in the sixties. However, he was and remained the most spiritual of the Beatles, composing marvelous songs like My Sweet Lord and Beware of Darkness, when he and Ravi Shankar organized the Concert for Bangladesh.

Now let's do Master Cheiro's Life Path Number; As you already know, he was born on November 1, 1866

Month 2 (November) = 11=2
Day is a 1
Year 1866 - 1+8+6+6 =3
Total the 3 lines - 2+1+3=6

Number 6 for Master Cheiro is quite appropriate when you consider the 6's potential for self destruction under certain circumstances. A 6 can be despondent

Now let's do your Life Path Number;

Month	
Day	
Year	
Total	

Life Path Number Interpretations

The following pages define various vibrations of the momentum of your life; As with everything in life each thing has attributes of good and bad, nothing is absolute. There are no good or bad numbers. All numbers have positive and negative aspects in them. A seven is not always lucky of the thirteen is not always unlucky. The Chaldean system places special emphasis on auspicious and not auspicious days, months, bringing it more aligned with Astrology.

The Number 1 (Life Path)

The number one "1" stands in this symbolism for the Sun. It is the beginning-that by which all the rest of the nine numbers were created. The basis of all numbers is one-the basis of all life is one.

This number represents all that is creative, individual, and positive. Without going into further details, a person born under the Birth number of 1, or any of its series, has the underlying principles of being in his or her work creative, inventive, strongly individual, definite in his or her views, and in consequence more or less obstinate and determined in all they as individuals undertake. This relates to all men and women born under the number 1, such as on the first, 10th, 19th, or 28th of any month (the addition of all these numbers making a 1), but more especially so if they happen to be born between the 21st July and the 28th August, which is the period of the Zodiac called the" House of the Sun," or from the 21st March to the 28th April, when the Sun enters the Vernal Equinox and is considered elevated or all-powerful during this period.

It is for this reason, which you will observe has a logical basis, that people born under the number "1" in these particular periods must have the qualities that I have given to all number "1" people in a distinctly more marked degree.

Let us read about qualities of Number "1" people;

General Characteristics

Number 1 people are ambitious; they dislike restraint, they always rise in whatever their profession or occupation may be. They desire to become the heads of whatever their businesses are, and as departmental chiefs they keep their authority and make themselves respected and" looked up to" by their subordinates. The positive aspect of this number are;

a Leader, pioneer but it can also become selfish, lazy, egocentric with destructive connotation of dictatorial, maniacal, or power hungry.

Auspicious Dates & Days

These number 1[7] people should strive to carry out their most important plans and ideas on all days that vibrate to their own number, such as on the 1st, 10th, 19th, or 28th of any month, but especially in those periods I have described before, namely, from the 21st July to the 28th August, and from the 21st March to the 28th April. Outside of their own numbers, number 1 people get on well with persons born under the 2, 4, and 7, such as those born on the 2nd, 4th, 7th, 11th, 13th, 16th, 20th, , 22nd, 25th, 29th, and 31st, especially those born in the strong periods indicated. The days of the week most fortunate for number "1" persons are Sunday and Monday, and especially so if one of their "own numbers" should also fall on that day, such as the 1st, 10th, 19th, or 28th, and next to that their interchangeable numbers of 2, 4, 7, such as the 2nd, 4th, 7th, 11th, 13th, 16th, 20th, 22nd, 25th, 29th, or 31st.

Favorable Colors and Jewels

The most fortunate colors for persons born under the number "1" are all shades of gold, yellows and bronze to golden brown. Their "lucky" jewels are the topaz, amber, yellow diamond and all stones of these colors. If possible, they should wear a piece of amber next their flesh.

The Number 2 (Life Path)

The number 2 stands in symbolism for the Moon. It has the feminine attributes of the Sun, and, for this reason alone, although number 1 and number 2 people are decidedly opposite in their characters, their vibrations are harmonious and they make good combinations. Number 2 people are all those who are born on the 2nd, 11th, 20th, or 29th in any month, but their characteristics are the more marked if they are born between the 20th June and the 27th July, this period being what is called the "House of the Moon."

I have added the seven days of the "Cusp" to the 20th July. Number 2 persons and number 1 vibrate together, and in a lesser degree with number 7 people, such as those born on the 7th, 16th, or 25th in any month.

Let us read about qualities of Number "2" people.

---

[7] this mainly pertains to your Life Path number (not the date of birth

General Characteristics

Number 2 persons are gentle by nature, imaginative, artistic, and romantic. Like the number 1 people, they are also inventive, but they are not as forceful in carrying out their ideas. Their qualities are more on the mental than the physical plane and they are seldom as strong physically as those born under the number 1.

The chief faults they should guard against are-being restless and unsettled, lack of continuity in their plans and ideas, and lack of self-confidence. They are also inclined to be oversensitive, and too easily get despondent and melancholy if they are not in happy surroundings. The positive aspect of this number are;

Cooperative and considerate, very adaptable but it can also become subservient, shy, indifferent with destructive connotation of dishonest, cruel, or pessimistic.

Auspicious Dates & Days

Number 2 (Life Path persons) should strive to carry out their chief plans and ideas on days whose numbers vibrate with their own, such as on the 2nd, 11th, 20th, or 29th of any month, but more especially during the period of the 20th June to the 27th July. The days of the week more fortunate or "lucky" for them are Sunday, Monday, and Friday (the reason Friday is favorable in this case is that it is governed by Venus), and especially so if, like the number 1 people, one of their own numbers should fall on either of these days, such as the 2nd, 11th, 20th, or 29th, and next to these their interchangeable numbers of 1, 4, 7, such as the 1st, 4th, 7th, 10th, 13th, 16th, 19th, 22nd, 25th, 28th, or 31St.

Favorable Colors and Jewels

Colors they should wear all shades of green, from the darkest to the lightest, also cream and white, but as far as possible they should avoid all dark colors, especially black, purple, and dark red.

Their" lucky" stones and jewels are pearls, moonstones, pale green stones, and they should carry a piece of jade always with them, and, if possible, next to their skin .

The Number 3 (Life Path)

The number 3 stands in symbolism for the Planet Jupiter, a Planet which plays a most important role both in Astrology and in all systems of Numerology. It is the beginning of what may be termed one of the main lines of force that runs right through all the numbers from 3 to 9. It has a special relation to every third in the series, such as 3, 6, 9, and all their additions. These numbers added together in any direction produce a 9 as their final digit, and the 3, 6, 9 people are all sympathetic to one another. Persons having a 3 for their Birth number are all those who are born on the 3rd, 12th, 21st, or 30th in any month, but the number 3 has still more significance if they should be born in what is called the" period of the 3," from the 19th February to March 20th-27th, or from the 21st November to December 20th-27th.

Let us read about qualities of Number "3" people;

General Characteristics

Number 3 people, like the number 1 individuals, are decidedly ambitious; they are never satisfied by being in subordinate positions; their aim is to rise in the world, to have control and authority over others. They are excellent in the execution of commands; they love order and discipline in all things; they readily obey orders themselves, but they also insist on having their orders obeyed.

Number 3 people often rise to the very highest positions in any business, profession or sphere in which they may be found. They often excel in positions of authority in the army and navy, in government, and in life generally; and especially in all posts of trust and responsibility, as they are extremely conscientious in carrying out their duties.

Their faults are that they are inclined to be dictatorial, to "lay down the law" and to insist on carrying out their own ideas. For this reason, although they are not quarrelsome, they succeed in making many enemies. Number 3 people are singularly proud; they dislike being under a compliment to others; they are also exceptionally independent, and chafe under the least restraint. The positive aspect of this number are;

Pleasant and charming, very optimistic but it can also become vain, shallow, self-conscious with destructive connotation of jealous, intolerant, or hypocritical.

Auspicious Dates & Days

Number 3 (Life Path persons) should strive to carry out their plans and aims on all days that vibrate to their own number, such as on the 3rd, 12th, 21st, and 30th of any month, but more especially when these dates fall in the" period of the 3," such as from the 19th February to March 20th-27th, and from the 21st November to December 20th-27th. The days of the week more" lucky" for them are Thursday, Friday, and Tuesday; Thursday being the most important. These days are especially good if a number making a 3 should fall on it, such as the 3rd, 12th, 21st, or 30th, and next in order their interchangeable numbers of 6 and 9 such as the 6th, 9th, 15th, 18th, 24th, or 27th. Number 3 people are more in harmony with those born under their own number or under the 6 and 9, such as all those who are born on a 3rd, 12th, 21st, 30th. 6th, 15th, 24th. 9th, 18th, 27th.

Favorable Colors and Jewels

For" lucky" colors they should wear some shade of mauve, violet, or purple, or some touch of these colors should always be with them; also in the rooms in which they live. All shades of blue, crimson, and rose are also favorable to them, but more as secondary colors. Their" lucky" stone is the amethyst. They should always have one on their persons, and if possible, wear it next their skin.

The Number 4 (Life Path)

The number 4 stands in its symbolism for the Planet Uranus. It is considered related to the Sun, number 1, and in occultism is written as 4-1. Number 4 people are all those who are born on the 4th, 13th, 22nd, and 31st in any month; their individuality is still more pronounced if they are born in the Zodiacal period of the Sun and Moon, namely, between the 21st June and July 20th-27th (Moon period) and from the 21st July to the end of August (Sun period).

Let us read about qualities of Number "4" people.

General Characteristics

Number 4 people have a distinct character of their own. They appear to view everything from an opposite angle to everyone else. In an argument they will always take the opposite side, and although not meaning to be quarrelsome, yet they bring about opposition and make a great number of secret enemies who constantly work against them. They seem quite naturally to take a different view of anything that is presented to their minds. They instinctively rebel against rules and regulations, and if they can have their way they reverse the order of things, even in communities and governments. They often rebel against constitutional authority and set up new rules and regulations either in domestic or public life. They are inclined to be attracted to social questions and reforms of all kinds, and are very positive and unconventional in their views and opinions. Number 4 people do not make friends easily. They seem more attracted to persons born under the 1, 2, 7 and 8 numbers. They are seldom as successful in worldly or material matters as people born under the other numbers, and as a rule they are more or less indifferent as to the accumulation of wealth. If they do acquire money or have it given to them they generally surprise people by the way they employ it or the use they put it to.

Their chief faults are that they are most highly strung and sensitive, very easily wounded in their feelings, inclined to feel lonely and isolated, and are likely to become despondent and melancholy unless they have achieved success. As a rule they make few real friends, but to the few they have, they are most devoted and loyal, but are always inclined to take the part of "the under-dog" in any argument or any cause they espouse. The positive aspect of this number are;

Master Organizer and pragmatism, very exact but it can also become meddlesome, penurious, rigid with destructive connotation of ruthless, vulgar, or even violent.

Auspicious Dates & Days

Number 4 Life Path folks should strive to carry out their plans and ideas on all days that have their number 4, such as the 4th, 13th, 22nd, and 31st of any month, but especially so if these dates come in their strong period, from the 21st June to July 20th-27th, or from the 22nd July to the end of August. The days of the week more fortunate or "lucky" for them are Saturday, Sunday, and Monday, especially so if their" own number" should fall on one of these days, such as the 4th, 13th, 22nd, or 31st, and next in order their interchangeable numbers of 1, 2, 7, such as the 1st, 2nd, 7th, 10th, 11th, 16th, 19th, 20th, 25th, 28th, or 29th.

Favorable Colors and Jewels

For "lucky" colors, they should wear what are called "half-shades," "half-tones," or "electric colors." "Electric blues" and greys seem to suit them best of all. Their" lucky" stone is the sapphire, light or dark, and if possible they should wear this stone next their skin.

The Number 5 (Life Path)

The number 5 stands in symbolism for the Planet Mercury, and is versatile and mercurial in all its characteristics. Number 5 people are all those who are born on the 5th, 14th, and 23rd in any month, but their characteristics are still more marked if they are born in what is called the "period of the 5," which is from the 21st May to June 20th-27th, and from the 21st August to September 20th 27th.

Let us learn about the Qualities of Number 5 People.

General Characteristics

Number 5 people make friends easily and get on with persons born under almost any other number, but their best friends are those who are born under their own number, such as the 5th, 14th, and 23rd of any month. Number 5 people are mentally very highly strung. They live on their nerves and appear to crave excitement. They are quick in thought and decisions, and impulsive in their actions. They detest any plodding kind of work and seem naturally to drift into all methods of making money quickly. They have a keen sense of making money by inventions and new ideas. They are born speculators, prone to Stock Exchange transactions, and generally are willing and ready to run risks in all they undertake. They have the most wonderful elasticity of character. They rebound quickly from the heaviest blow; nothing seems to affect them for very long; like their symbol, quicksilver, which Mercury represents, the blows of Fate leave no indentations on their character. If they are by nature good they remain so; if bad, not all the preaching in the world will make the slightest effect on them. Weakness of number 5 people Their greatest drawback is that they exhaust their nervous strength to such an extent that they often fall victims to nervous breakdowns of the worst kind, and under any mental tension they easily become irritable and quick-tempered, unable to "suffer fools gladly." The positive aspect of this number are;

Versatile and adventurous, progressive but it can also become Sensationalistic, untrustworthy, uncultured with destructive connotation of perverse, overindulgent, with a penchant of dependency of drugs and alcohol.

Favorable Dates & Days

Number 5 people should strive to carry out their plans and aims on all days that fall under their" own number," such as the 5th, 14th, or 23rd of any month, but more especially when these dates fall in the" period of the 5," namely from the 21st May to June 20th-27th, or from the 21st August to September 20th-27th. The days of the week more fortunate or "lucky" for them are Wednesday and Friday, especially if their" own number" falls on one of these days.

Favorable Colors and Jewels

Their" lucky" colors are all shades of light grey, white, and glistening materials, but just as they can make friends with people born under all kinds of numbers, so can they wear all shades of colors, but by far the best for them are light shades, and they should wear dark colors as rarely as possible. Their" lucky" stone is the diamond, and all glittering or shimmering things; also ornaments made of platinum or silver, and, if possible, they should wear a diamond set in platinum next their skin.

The Number 6 (Life Path)

The number 6 stands in symbolism for the Planet Venus. Persons having a 6 as their Birth number are all those who are born on the 6th, 15th, or 24th of any month, but they are more especially influenced by , this number if they are born in what is called the" House of the 6," which is from the 20th April to May 20th-27th, and from the 21st September to October 20th-27th.

As a rule all number 6 people are extremely magnetic; they attract others to them, and they are loved and often worshipped by those under them.

Let us learn about the Qualities of Number 6 People.

General Characteristics

They are very determined in carrying out their plans, and may, in fact, be deemed obstinate and unyielding, except when they themselves become deeply attached: in such a case they become devoted slaves to those they love. Although number 6 people are considered influenced by the Planet Venus, yet as a rule theirs is more the" mother love" than the sensual. They lean to the romantic and ideal in all matters of the affections. In some ways they take very strongly after the supposed qualities of Venus, in that they love beautiful things, they make most artistic homes, are fond of rich colors, also paintings, statuary, and music. If rich they are most generous to art and artists, they love to entertain their friends and make everyone happy about them, but the one thing they cannot stand is discord and jealousy. When roused by anger they will brook no opposition, and will fight to the death for whatever person or cause they espouse, or out of their sense of duty. The number 6 people have got the power of making more friends than any other class, with the exception of the number 5, but especially so with all persons born under the vibration of the 3, the 6, the 9, or all their series. The positive aspect of this number are;

Harmony and domesticity, balanced but it can also become egotistical and unreasonable, also blunt and despondent with destructive connotation of tyrannical, paranoid.

Favorable Dates & Days

Their most important days in the week are Tuesdays, Thursdays, and Fridays, and especially so if a number of 3, 6, or 9, such as the 3rd, 6th, 9th, 12th, 15th, 18th, 21st, 24th, 27th, or 30th, should fall on one of those days. Number 6 people should strive to carry out their plans and aims on all dates that fall under their" own number," such as the 6th, 15th, or 24th of any month, but more especially when these dates fall in the" period of the 6," namely, between the 20th April and May 20th-27th, or from the 21st September to October 20th-27th.

Favorable Colors and Jewels

Their" lucky" colors are all shades of blue, from the lightest to the darkest, also all shades of rose or pink, but they should avoid wearing black or dark purple. Their" lucky" stone is especially the turquoise, and, as far as possible, they should wear one, or a piece of turquoise matrix, next their skin. Emeralds are also" lucky" for the number 6 people.

The Number 7 (Life Path)

THE number 7 stands in symbolism for the Planet Neptune, and represents all persons born under the 7, namely those who are born on the 7th, 16th, or 25th of any month, but more especially influences such persons if they were born from the 21st June to July 20th-27th, the period of the Zodiac called the" House of the Moon." The Planet Neptune has always been considered as associated with the Moon, and, as the part. of the Zodiac I have mentioned is also called the First' House of Water, the connection of Neptune whose very name is always associated with Water is then logical and easily understood. Now, as the number of the Moon is always given as a 2, this explains why it is that the number 7 people have as their secondary number the 2, and get on well and make friends easily with all those born under the Moon numbers, namely, the 2nd, 11th, 20th, and 29th of any month, especially so if they are also born in the" House of the Moon," from the 21st of June to the end of July.

Let us learn about the Qualities of Number 7 People.

General Characteristics

People born under the number 7, namely, on the 7th, 16th, or 25th of any month, are very independent, original, and have strongly marked individuality. At heart they love change and travel, being restless in their natures. If they have the means of gratifying their desires they visit foreign countries and become keenly interested in the affairs of far-off lands. They devour books on travel and have a wide universal knowledge of the world at large. They often make extremely good writers, painters, or poets, but in everything they do, they sooner or later show a peculiar philosophical outlook on life that tinges all their work. As a class they care little about the material things of life; they often become rich by their original ideas or methods of business, but if they do they are just as likely to make large donations from their wealth to charities or institutions. The women of this number generally marry well, as they are always anxious about the future, and feel that they need some rock to rest on lest the waters of Fate sweep them away. The number 7 people have good ideas about business, or rather their plans are good if they will only carry them out. They have usually a keen desire to travel and read a great deal about far-off countries. If they can they will become interested in matters concerning the sea, and in trade or business they often become merchants, exporters and importers, dealing with foreign countries, and owners or captains of ships if they can get the chance. Number 7 people have very peculiar ideas about religion. They dislike to follow the beaten track; they create a religion of their own, but one that appeals to the imagination and based on the mysterious. These people usually have remarkable dreams and. a great leaning to occultism; they have the gift of intuition, clairvoyance, and a peculiar quieting magnetism of their own that has great influence over others. The positive aspect of this number are;

Wisdom and insightful, introspective but it can also become weird, aloof, rebellious with destructive connotation of repressed, deceitful, with a penchant of becoming flakey.

Favorable Dates & Days

Number 7 people should strive to carry out their plans and aims on all days that fall under their" own number," such as the 7th, 16th, or 25th of any month, but more especially when these dates fall in the" period of the 7," namely, from the 21st June to July 20th-27th-and less strongly from that date to the end of August. The days of the week more fortunate or "lucky" for them are the same as for the number 2 people, namely, Sunday and Monday, especially if their" own number" falls on one of these days, or their interchangeable numbers of 1, 2, 4, such as the 1st, 2nd, 4th, l0th, 11th, 13th, 19th, 20th, 22nd, 28th, 29th, or 31st.

Lucky Colors and Jewels

Their" lucky" colors are all shades of green, pale shades, also white and yellow, and they should avoid all heavy dark colors as much as possible. Their" lucky" stones are moonstones, "cat's-eyes," and pearls, and if possible, they should wear a moonstone or a piece of moss agate next their skin.

The Number 8 (Life Path)

The number 8 stands in symbolism for the Planet Saturn. This number influences all persons born on the 8th, 17th, or 26th in any month, but still more so if their birthday comes between the 21st December and the 26th January, which period is called the House of Saturn (Positive), and from the 26th . January to February 19th-26th, the period called the House of Saturn (Negative). These people are invariably much misunderstood in their lives, and perhaps for this reason they feel intensely lonely at heart.

Let us learn about the Qualities of Number 8 People.

General Characteristics

These people are invariably much misunderstood in their lives, and perhaps for this reason they feel intensely lonely at heart. They have deep and very intense natures, great strength of individuality; they generally play some important role on life's stage, but usually one which is fatalistic, or as the instrument of Fate for others. If at all religious they go to extremes and are fanatics in their zeal. In any cause they take up, they attempt to carry it through in spite of all argument or opposition, and in doing so they generally make bitter and relentless enemies. They often appear cold and undemonstrative, though in reality they have warm hearts towards the oppressed, of all classes; but they hide their feelings and allow people to think just what they please. These number 8 people are either great successes or great failures; there appears to be no happy medium in their case.

If ambitious, they generally aim for public life or government responsibility of some kind, and often hold very high positions involving great sacrifice on their part. It is not, however, from a worldly standpoint, a fortunate number to be born under, and such persons often are called on to face the very greatest sorrows, losses, and humiliations. The positive aspect of this number are;

Strong personality and self-control, a leader but it can also become selfish, power hungry, self-serving with destructive connotation of being miserly, abusive and unjust.

Favorable Dates & Days

The number 8 being a Saturn number, Saturday is therefore their most important day, but on account of the number 4 having influence on a Sunday and in a secondary way on a Monday, the number 8 people will find Saturday, Sunday, and Monday their most important days. Number 8 people should strive to carry out their plans and aims on all days that fall under their" own number," such as the 8th, 17th, or 26th in any month, but more especially so when these dates fall in the" period of the 8," namely, from the 21st December to January 20th-27th, and from that date to February 19th-26th; also if these dates fall on a Saturday, Sunday, or Monday, or their interchangeable number, which is 4, such as the 4th, 13th, 22nd, or 31st.

Favorable Colors and Jewels

The" lucky" colors for people born under the 8 are all shades of dark grey, black, dark blue, and purple. If number 8 persons were to dress in light colors they would look awkward, and as if there were something wrong with them. Their "lucky" stones are the amethyst and the dark toned sapphire, also the black pearl or the black diamond, and if possible they should wear one of these next their skin.

The number 8 is a difficult number to explain. It represents two worlds, the material and the spiritual. It is in fact, if one regards it, like two circles just touching together. It is composed of two equal numbers: 4 and 4. From the earliest ages it has been associated with the symbol of an irrevocable Fate, both in connection with the lives of individuals or nations. In Astrology it stands for Saturn, which is also called the Planet of Fate. One side of the nature of this number represents upheaval, revolution, anarchy, waywardness and eccentricities of all kinds. The other side represents philosophic thought, a strong leaning towards occult studies, religious devotion, concentration of purpose, zeal for any cause espoused, and a fatalistic outlook coloring all actions. All persons who have the number 8 clearly associated with their lives feel that they are distinct and different from their fellows. At heart they are lonely; they are misunderstood, and they seldom reap the reward for the good they may do while they are living. After their death they are often extolled, their works praised, and lasting tributes offered to their memory. Those on the lower plane generally come into conflict with human justice and have some tragic ending to their lives. Those on the higher plane carry their misunderstood motives and lay bare the tragedy of their souls before Divine Justice. To distinguish in which of these two classes a number 8 person falls, one must find by the comparison of their "fadic" numbers if they are completely dominated by the recurrence of 8 in the principal events of their lives, or if some other equally powerful number such as the 1, 3 or 6 series does not more or less balance the sequel of events registered under the 8 and all its series. If the latter is the case, one may be sure that by the long series of reincarnations they have passed through, they have paid the price in some former state, and are now passing towards the higher, where Divine Justice will give them their reward. If, on the contrary, we find that the person is completely dominated by the number 8, always recurring in important events, or if instead of 8 the nearly equally fatalistic number of 4 is continually recurring, we may then be sure that we are in the presence of one of those strange playthings of Fate with the possibilities that tragedy may be interwoven in their Destiny. In the more ordinary tragedies of everyday life, we can find an illuminating example in the life and execution of Crippen[8], whose principal actions were singularly influenced by the terrible combination of the 8 and the 4. Looking back over his career, and especially the events which led up to his paying that terrible forfeit at the hands of the law, one will find these numbers associated in the most dramatic way with this man's life, as illustrated by the following facts: The figures of the year he was born in (1862), if added together, produce an 8 (17 equals I plus 7 equals 8). He was born on the 26th of January, or 2 plus 6 equals 8. His wife was not seen alive after dinner with him on the 31st January, which is a 4, and the month of January is itself called the House of Saturn, whose number is an 8. He made his statement to Inspector Drew (which was later to be used as overwhelming evidence against him) on the 8th July. The human remains were found in the cellar on 13th July, which again makes the number 4. To try to escape he chose the name "Robinson," which has, strange to say, 8 letters in it. He was recognized on board the Montrose on the 22nd July, which again equals a 4. The name of the ship he chose to leave Europe by (the Montrose) has 8 letters, and the ship that brought him back to his doom, the Megantic, was also composed of 8 letters. He was arrested, as this ship reached Canada, on the morning of the 31st July, which again equals 4. His trial finished on Saturday, 22nd October, which is again the 4, and October being the month of "the detriment of Saturn" gives again the 8. The occult number by which Saturday is designated is an 8. His execution was fixed for the 8th November. His appeal was heard and refused on Saturday, 5th November. The 5 added to the 8, which Saturday is a symbol of, again makes the figure 13, which number again equals a 4. When his appeal failed, the date of execution was changed to the 23rd November.

The addition of 2-3 makes a 5, and the division of the Zodiac which represents this portion of November is designated as a 3; and this 3, if added to the date (the 23rd), makes the figure 26, which by addition (2 plus 6) again equals 8. Or if the 3 were added to the number of 23 we would get 26 or the 8. The symbol of the number 8, I may also mention, from time immemorial, in occult studies, is called the" symbol of human justice." Lastly, when Crippen's" Key numbers" the 4 and 8, came together, it was the fatal year of his life. He was 48 years old when executed.

It is not my province to judge or condemn this unfortunate being. Crippen, in any case, suffered as few men have been called upon to suffer; but I may add that the. combination of such numbers as 4 and 8 as the" Key numbers" in any life, indicate an individual terribly under the influence of Fate, and one especially unfortunate through his or her affections.

I have followed out many cases of people having similar "Key numbers," and in every case they seem sooner or later to come into conflict with what the 8 represents, namely, the

---

[8] Hawley Harvey Crippen (September 11, 1862 —November 23, 1910), usually known as Dr. Crippen, was an American homeopath, ear and eye specialist and medicine dispenser. He was hanged in Pentonville Prison for the murder of his wife Cora Henrietta Crippen, and was the first criminal to be captured with the aid of wireless telegraphy.

symbol of "human justice." They are generally condemned, even in ordinary social life, by the weight of circumstantial evidence, and they usually die with their secret, appealing, as it were, from the sentence of "human justice," which, as a rule, has been against them, to that of the Divine Justice in the world beyond. The occult symbol of 8 has from time immemorial been represented by the figure of Justice with a Sword pointing upwards and a Balance or Scales in the left hand. There are many very curious things in history as regards this number.

The Greeks called it the number of Justice on account of its equal divisions of equally even numbers. The Jews practiced circumcision on the 8th day after birth. At their Feast of Dedication they kept 8 candles burning, and this Feast lasted 8 days. Eight prophets were descended from Rahab. There were 8 sects of Pharisees.

Noah was the 8th in direct descent from Adam. The strange number of three eights (888) is considered by students of Occultism to be the number of Jesus Christ in His aspect as the Redeemer of the world.

Curiously enough, the addition of 888 makes 24 and 2 plus 4 gives the 6 which is the number of Venus, the representative of Love. This number 888 given to Christ is in direct opposition to 666 which Revelation says" is the number of the Beast or the number of Man." The numbers 666 if added together gives 18 (I plus 8 equals 9). This 9 is the number of Mars, the symbol of War, destruction, and force, which is decidedly the opposition of the 6 with the symbol of Love.

The Number 9 (Life Path)

The number 9 stands in symbolism for the Planet Mars. This number influences all persons born on the 9th, 18th, and 27th of any month, but still more so if their birthday falls in the period between the 21st March and April 19th-26th (called the House of Mars Positive) or in the period between the 21st October and November 20th-27th (called the House of Mars Negative).

This number 9 has some very curious properties. It is the only number in calculation that, multiplied by any number, always reproduces itself, as for example 9 times 2 is 18, and 8 plus I becomes again the 9, and so on with every number it is multiplied by.

It is, perhaps, not uninteresting to notice that : At the 9th day the ancients buried their dead. At the 9th hour the Jesus died on the Cross. The Romans held a feast in memory of their dead every 9th year. In some of the Hebrew writings it is taught that God has 9 times descended to this earth: 1St in the Garden of Eden, 2nd at the confusion of tongues at Babel, 3rd at the destruction of Sodom and Gomorrah, 4th to Moses at Horeb, 5th at Sinai when the Ten Commandments were given, 6th to Balaam, 7th to Elisha, 8th in the Tabernacle, 9th in the Temple at Jerusalem, and it is taught that at the 10th coming this earth will pass away and a new one will be created. Both the First and Second Temples of the Jews were destroyed on the 9th day of the Jewish month called Ab. On the 9th day of Ab, Jews who follow their religion cannot wear the Talith and Phylacteries until the Sun has set. There are so many curious things connected with the number 9 that it would not be possible to deal with one half of them in this description. For all purposes of occult calculation the numbers 7 and 9 are considered the most important of all.

The 7 has always been understood to relate to the spiritual plane, acting as the God or creative force on the Earth, and being creative, it is the uplifting" urge" towards the higher development of the spiritual in humanity. The 9 on the contrary, being, in the Planetary World, the representative of the Planet Mars, is the number of physical force in every form, and consequently stands in relation to the material.

When this explanation is carefully considered it throws an illuminating light on that mysterious text in Revelation, chapter xiii. verse 18: "Here is wisdom. Let him that hath understanding count the number of the beast, for it is the number of man, and his number is 666." This strange text has puzzled the theological mind for centuries, yet if you will take the trouble to add 666 together you will get 18, and 1 plus 8 gives you the figure 9, which in turn represents the 9 Planets of our Solar System, the 9 numbers upon which man builds all his calculations, and beyond which he cannot go except by continual repetition of the numbers I to 9. "6 6 6" producing its" spirit number" (as explained in the preceding page) of 9 is therefore, in all truth as Revelation states, "the number of man." The hidden meaning of this number is one of the greatest secrets of occultism, and has been concealed in a thousand ways, just as the cryptic text in Revelation has hidden it for centuries from the minds of Theologians. The number 9 representing man and everything to do with the physical and material plane, is the number of force, energy, destruction and war in its most dominant quality. In its relation to ordinary life it denotes energy, ambition, leadership, domination. It represents iron, the metal from which the weapons of warfare are made, and the Planet Mars which it stands for in Astrology is the Ruler of the Zodiacal Sign Aries which is the Sign of the Zodiac which governs England.

This symbolism was evidently well known by Shakespeare when he wrote" England, thou seat of Mars." The number 9 is an emblem of matter that can never be destroyed, so the number 9 when multiplied by any number always reproduces itself, no matter what the extent of the number is that has been employed. The Novendiale was a fast in the Roman Catholic Church to avert calamities, and from this came the Roman Catholic system of Neuvaines. In Freemasonry there is an Order of "Nine Elected Knights," and in the working of this Order 9 roses, 9 lights and 9 knocks must be used. All ancient races encouraged a fear of the number 9, and all its multiples. The number 9 is considered a fortunate number to be born under, provided the man or woman does not ask for a peaceful or monotonous life, and can control their nature in not making enemies.

General Characteristics

Number 9 persons are 'fighters in all they attempt in life. They usually have difficult times in their early years, but generally they are, in the end, successful by their grit, strong will, and determination. , In character, they are hasty in temper, impulsive, independent, and desire to be their own masters. When the number 9 is noticed to be more than usually dominant in the dates and events of their lives they will be found to make great enemies, to cause strife and opposition wherever they may be, and they are often wounded or killed either in warfare or in the battle of life. They have great courage and make excellent soldiers or leaders in any cause they espouse. Their greatest dangers arise from foolhardiness and impulsiveness in word and action. They are also peculiarly prone to accidents from fire and explosions, and rarely get through life without injury, from such causes. As a general rule they go under many operations by the surgeon's knife. They usually experience many quarrels and strife in their home life, either with their own relations or with the family they marry into. They strongly resent criticism, and even when not conceited, they have always a good opinion of themselves, brooking no interference with their plans. They like to be "looked up to" and recognized as "the head of the house. " They are resourceful and excellent in organization, but they must have the fullest control; if not, they lose heart and stand aside and let things go to pieces. For affection and sympathy they will do almost anything, and the men of this number can be made the greatest fools of, if some clever woman gets pulling at their heartstrings. The positive aspect of this number are;

Compassionate and altruistic, spiritual but it can also become overly emotional, unstable, impractical with destructive connotation of bitterness, depressed.

Favorable Dates & Days

As a rule they get on best with persons whose birth date is one of the series of 3, 6, or 9, such as those born on the 3rd, 6th, 9th, 12th, 15th, 18th, 21st, 24th, 27th, or 30th of any month. All these numbers are in harmonious vibration to the number 9 people. Their most important days in the week are Tuesday, Thursday, and Friday, but more especially Tuesday (called Mars Day). Number 9 people should strive to carry out their plans and aims on all days that fall under their" own number," such as the 9th, 18th, or 27th in any month, but more especially when these dates fall in the" period of the 9," between the 21st March and April 19th-26th, or from the 21st October to November 20th-27th. And when the 9th,

18th, or 27th falls on their" own day," as mentioned above, or one of their interchangeable numbers which are the 3 and 6, such as the 3rd, 6th, 12th, 15th, 21st, 24th, and 30th.

Favorable Colors and Jewels

The" lucky[9]" colors for persons born under the number 9 are all shades of crimson or red, also all rose tones and pink. Their" lucky" stones are the ruby, garnet, and bloodstone, and they should wear one of these stones next their skin. This number is supposed to be a fortunate one to be born under, provided one controls it and is not carried away by the excesses of temper and violence that it also represents.

Life's Three Stages
Everyone's life can be broken up to at least three segments;

• the formative years - these are the times when you are most dependent on others; you are malleable, impressionable but daring and carefree and hopefully happy. Your whole life is ahead of you. This period is usually from birth to 28-35 years of age. Even people who suffer hardships during this time often reminisce about it with nostalgia of the magic of youth.

• The productive years - when you start earning, saving and accumulating assets. Ideally, you would end up working in a profession that is suitable to you and fulfilling. This is the time to settle down, start a family. This is often stressful because you take care of your kids and often your parents at the same time.

• Wisdom years - Hopefully you can slow down now on accumulating and see beyond this lifetime. You seek philosophy and ask questions. Your true self comes to the surface and in your wisdom years you try to understand the meaning of life understanding that life is a journey to learn past lives mistakes.

The next two chapters we shall look at two specific sub-cycles in your life-path.

---

[9] luck is a misused work, I prefer favorable. If it is mean to be certain days are better for accomplishing what is meant to be. Paradoxically, not all that is "meant to be" happens because of interference and personal choices we make.

Challenge Cycles

The Challenge numbers are significant in pointing our of what characteristic you lack in a certain period of your life. For example, as number 8 is a "money" number, if you have a challenge of your formidable years as number 8, it may indicate a serious lack of maturity in dealing with money. Irresponsible spending or taking too many risks might be another way of putting it.

When you have a Challenge number of zero it does not mean that you do not face some deficiency but this type of a challenge is not as severe. Typically this may indicate the need to seek your main purpose and goals in life.

Here is how to calculate your Challenge numbers.

It is worth noting that the Challenge number is one of the few areas of numerology in which subtraction is used. It is derived from your date of birth, using the month, the day, and the year, in that order.

To find your Challenges, use the following formula. I will use an example to make the steps easier to understand.

In our example of George Harrison, born February 25 1943 (2/25/1943), we reduce each of these units (the month, the day, and the year) to single digits. The result is 2, 7, 8.

To find the First Challenge we subtract the month of birth from the day of birth, or vice versa. In our example, we subtract 2 from 7 = 3.

The Second Challenge results from subtracting the day of birth from the year of birth, or vice versa. In our example, we deduct 7 from 8 = 1.

The Third and *main* Challenge is found by subtracting the First and Second Challenge, or vice versa. In our example, 3 - 1 = 2.

The Fourth Challenge is found by subtracting the month of birth from the year of birth, or vice versa. In our example, we deduct 2 from 8 = 6.

The time span of the Challenges:

THE FIRST CHALLENGE
The duration of the First Challenge usually lasts from birth until approximately the age of 30 to 35.
THE SECOND CHALLENGE
The Second Challenge usually lasts until the age of about 35 to 55/60.
THE THIRD CHALLENGE

This Challenge carries much weight and will be present throughout your life. For that reason, it is also called the Main Challenge.

As you master this challenge, your life will come more and more under your own control. You will incorporate the positive aspects of the challenge into your character. This is it's purpose in the first place. Therefore, there is implicit in the challenge a chance for great reward.

In short, this may be the secret to your success.

THE FOURTH CHALLENGE

The Fourth Challenge is most strongly felt during the latter part of our lives, beginning at the age of approximately 55/60.

The table below shows the three stages for Challenge Cycles.

Life Path number	End of First, start of Second Period Cycle	End of Second, start of Third Period Cycle
1	26-27	53-54
2	25-26	52-53
3	33-34	60-61
4	32-33	59-60
5	31-32	58-59
6	30-31	57-58
7	29-30	56-57
8	28-29	55-56
9	27-28	54-55

The following vibrations are the interpretations of your challenges by numbers;

The Number 0 (Challenge)

This happens quite often, and it does not mean that you are free of life's curve-balls. It is simply a less demanding Challenge interpreted that you need to find a meaning in your life. A purpose a goal to fulfill. As Joseph Campbell had so eloquently put it in the Hero's Journey;

"find your bliss."

The Number 1 (Challenge)

One Challenge would indicate the need for more independence, be more assertive, stand on your own feet.

The Number 2 (Challenge)

The number Two Challenge would indicate the need to be more cooperative, considerate. Be the arbiter or peacemaker. Do not go out on your own. Surround yourself with like minded people and excel!

The Number 3 (Challenge)

Need for self expression. You are unsure and shy. Be more assertive!

The Number 4 (Challenge)

This challenge is all about work and laying a good foundation. You cannot build a solid house on quicksand.

The Number 5 (Challenge)

You have a fear of change. Do not be stuck in the mud, embrace a little change and look upon as adventure.

The Number 6 (Challenge)

You must learn to accept things and people as they are. Remember the serenity prayer? Have the wisdom to know what you can change and what you cannot.

The Number 7 (Challenge)

Often these are self imposed challenges based on overdoing something virtuous. Moderation should be even in monastic life. Relax, mingle. You are very spiritual and that can be interpreted as aloof, unfriendly by some.

The Number 8 (Challenge)

Be more responsible with finances, money, savings. Money is not the root of evil nor the key to happiness. It is simply a tool to advance our cause. You cannot take it with you but your kids or survivors could be benefited when you pass on.

The Number 9 (Challenge)

There is no such thing.

Pinnacle Cycles

The Pinnacle (or as some call it Attainment) cycles are your life path broken up and looked at its various chapters. As most great books are broken up into several parts, so is your life should be looked upon as you formative, early years.

To find your First Pinnacle, add the numbers of your month and day of birth, arriving at a single-digit number. For example, lets look at George Harrison birth date; 25 February 1943, his First Pinnacle would be found by adding the 2 (for February) and the 7 (for the twenty-five) to arrive at 9.

To find your Second Pinnacle, add the day you were born to the year of your birth. Using 25 February 1943 again, add the 7 (for the twenty-fifth day) and the birth year 8 (for 1943) and arrive at 15(1+5=6.)

To find your Third Pinnacle, add the sum of the first and the second Pinnacles - in our example, 9 plus 6 - and arrive at 15(1+5=6).

To find your Fourth and last Pinnacle, add your month and year of birth. Using the example, add 2 (for February) and 8 (for 1943) to arrive at 10, which reduces to 1.

The time span of Pinnacle cycles is as follows; the first Pinnacle is from birth to 33-35 year.

It is worth noting that only the military, voting or driving licenses consider a 21 year old person as a mature adult. Obviously, maturities vary but it is seldom that a person matures before age 27-28. Jesus was 33 years old when he was crucified and we do not know a lot from his early years. But what we know is that true creativity and adulthood comes after the first experimenting 27 formative years. The second and third Pinnacle Cycle last nine years each and the last, the Fourth Pinnacle cycle stays with you for the rest of your life.

Interestingly, the formula to determine our cusp is based on a formula three nine year cycle plus your Life Path Number. I'd guess the number one life path makes you mature a little more. This to me proves the divine providence of these old divination systems.

When there is a change in your Pinnacle cycle you will know it. Usually there is a cusp of two years before there is a change actually takes place.

The formula to use is based on - 36 minus the Life Path Number subtracted

	Your 1st Pinnacle Cycle starts at age:	Your 2nd Pinnacle Cycle starts at age:	Your 3rd Pinnacle Cycle starts at age: :	Your 4th Pinnacle Cycle starts at age:
Life path is 1	0 - 35	35-44	44-53	53+
Life Path is 2	0-34	34-43	43-52	52+
Life Path is 3	0-33	33-42	42-51	51+
Life Path is 4	0-32	32-41	41-50	50+
Life Path is 5	0-31	31-40	40-49	49+
Life Path is 6	0-30	30-39	39-48	48+
Life Path is 7	0-29	29-38	38-47	47+
Life Path is 8	0-28	28-37	37-46	46+
Life Path is 9	0-27	27-36	36-45	45+

Let us calculate the Pinnacle cycles for George Harrison, whose Life Path Number we already know is 8. So, the first Pinnacle Cycle is from age 0-27, which we already established as a 9. Just to recap from above. The second cycle was 6, the third was also 6 and the fourth was a 1.

The following are the interpretation of the Pinnacle numbers.

The Number 1 (Pinnacle)

Number one is hard in the early formative years because we are dependent on our parents or caretakers for years. You could be the teenage wizard of the stock market or some other creative venue. You must however temper your ego and cockiness.

Later, number one people seldom retire only they reinvent themselves, fully knowing that inactivity is not an option. It is unhealthy for the body and the mind. Patience and self understanding is a must.

The Number 2 (Pinnacle)

In the formative years you could be badly spoiled and impatient. If you grew up in a divorced family you must learn to adjust and manage. Later in life as part of the workforce you learn to attend to detail sometimes even micromanage. You are a party person greatly enjoying people at work and in your social circle. After retirement you could enjoy your family and friends.

The Number 3 (Pinnacle)

If you are in this cycle in the formative years then you must learn to express yourself in some venue. You could get interested in art or writing, story telling. Later in your work you will be most happy to use your creativity. Design, decorating, lecturing are all possibilities.
You will also find full retirement a burden and must continually reinvent yourself.

The Number 4 (Pinnacle)

Hard times at the formative years because schools are not the best place for you. Must learn the value of routine. Later in the workforce you will be applying the school learnt rudiments because by this time you will crave the daily routine. Be careful not to over do it.
In your later years do not look for retirement because either by choice or necessity you will be doing something. Self-employment is an option but you also learn to relax and enjoy some form of recreation.

The Number 5 (Pinnacle)

In the formative school years this cycle is about change and freedom. You could be restless and changing your mind, leaving unfinished projects. Impulsiveness and haphazard acts must be tempered and managed.
Because of your affinity towards the nature of change and movement your ideal job would be in the travel or hospitality industry, possibly in the police force of local or federal capacity. Be careful of drinking and gambling. In the later years you might be ambivalent whether you retire or not, if your health permits you might work or just change career.

The Number 6 (Pinnacle)

In the formative school years this cycle is about help and service. Even as a child you love to be needed and strive to situations that fulfill that. Home choirs are always done and without asking.

Because of your affinity service and responsibility financial rewards will come automatically if you find your bliss and do what you are supposed to do. Working with others comes naturally to your. In the later years you might end up doing volunteer work as you are not motivated by money but by ideals.

The Number 7 (Pinnacle)

In the formative years this person is usually misunderstood. Typically quite and introspective this person sometimes gets bullied by other kids. In the productive, working years opportunities would come when not soughed after. Lay back and let the Universe guide you. Things will happen when the time is right, and we often not aware of that. During the final chapter you are free from the productive pressures and can freely express yourself with philosophical matter and even at time the mystical, metaphysical, realizing that true learning never ends.

The Number 8 (Pinnacle)

In the formative years this person should be taught the principles of finances and money as early as possible. Money or actually mismanaging money will be an issue later and if proper emphasis is applied early this could alleviate later problems. In the productive, working years this person can focus on making the best of his/her skills. Earning a lot is important because usually expenses are going to be high. During the final chapter financial planning is still in the focus but good habits accustomed during earlier will help.

The Number 9 (Pinnacle)

In the formative years this person would face quite a few hardships because the perception of being unappreciated and unloved. The best way to handle this is with the understanding that the Universe is not picking on us personally. All is a result of our Karmic balance and each life is a blessing and an opportunity to learn and to strive to accumulate good Karma, thus shaping our future lives, at the present. With each special attribute such as a 9, we are also carry a little added weight, as all of our material existence is represented in polarity.

Light creates the shadow. Later in life, things tend to get better as a 9 usually understands Spirituality rather early and with the new-found knowledge comes salvation.

Happy Birth Day!

The date of birth is often celebrated in modern culture because of the often overlooked Numerological importance we include this chapter. Numerology is not just an curiosity subject, often dealt with the hidden skepticism and doubt, it should be practiced in daily life. As with all things with continuing practice, comes perfection.

In the early, curious phase you as a neophyte study the subject but do not practice it in your own life. In order for this magic to come alive (it would take time), but when and if this happens, you'd be embarking on doing important matters ONLY on auspicious days, if possible. Doing so, the secret of Numbers will further reveal themselves to you. But be patient, it all takes time.

Birth Day Vibrations

The calendar day hides secrets of your potential that should be viewed when looking for suitable professions, or fields of study.

The Number 1 (birthday)

Personal Traits (Remember, the color mixing example, a 10 has, to some extent all that the 1 has, but the emphasis and gradation is different) We list the more striking attributes when listing the various sub-numbers;)

1st Independent, entrepreneurial, practical with knowledge
10th Creative, not a homemaker, visionary
19th Has all traits of the above two but is subject to extremes
28th Independent with warmth, a Dreamer with a personality, strong willed

The Number 2 (birthday)

Personal Traits (the characteristic are shared and the list includes the predominant ones for example; a 2 can be strong willed but that is not the predominant feature for this sub-number.)

2nd Usually you are a core person of a group keeping it together
11th Inspirational, emotional
20th Tactful, good ear for music
29th Buoyant, a daydreamer, needy with family and friends alike

The Number 3 (birthday)

Personal Traits (the characteristic are shared and the list includes the predominant ones only;)

3rd   A people person, creative
12th Practical, logical
21st Social, nervous disposition
30th Imaginative, sedentary

The Number 4 (birthday)

Personal Traits (the characteristic are shared and the list includes the predominant ones only;)

4th   Systematic, detail oriented
13th hard worker, Lucky
22nd Universalist, Intuitive
31st Good feel for making money, determined

The Number 5 (birthday)

Personal Traits (the characteristic are shared and the list includes the predominant ones only;)

5th   Intuitive, versatile
14th Moody, Lucky
23rd Businesslike, quick-thinking

The Number 6 (birthday)

Personal Traits (the characteristic are shared and the list includes the predominant ones only;)

6th   Very local (community, home) oriented, musical
15th Generous, Sentimental
24th Good with older people, civic minded

The Number 7 (birthday)

Personal Traits (the characteristic are shared and the list includes the predominant ones only;)

7th   good chance that has a psychic gift, stubborn

16th Analytical, moody and can be needy

25th Intuitive, curious about the occult, lacks self-confidence

The Number 8 (birthday)

Personal Traits (the characteristic are shared and the list includes the predominant ones only;)

8th   potential for a successful business, good judge of intrinsic values.

17th Materialistic , set in his/her ways

26th Organized, high strung emotionally

The Number 9 (birthday)

Personal Traits (the characteristic are shared and the list includes the predominant ones only;)

9th   Internationalist, philanthropist.

18th Efficient, offers good advice

27th Multifaceted, forceful with good intuition.

Part II. Using the Letters of the Name

The Expression Number

In the olden days it was said that a child left without a name got sick and died. When having kids, it is our parental duty to give an identity to the new little person in this world. As parents we often agonize over names and combinations of names. There is so much magic and power in naming a child that in India[10], even today people consult professional Vedic numerologist to do the job right. Often the name carries so much weight that when a name change takes place, often it is coupled with a distinct personality change. It might take up to six month to a name change to take effect and it is often used by creative people and mystics alike.

The Expression Number or some call it Destiny is derived from you names given at birth. The name should be complete with middle name (if given) on the birth certificate.

Do not use titles or any given suffixes such as Corporation (when dealing with a business entity.) Junior or Jr. or any other such artificial additions should be ignored. Any clerical or typo is only accepted if the parents were using it as such and accepted it for the child. During mass immigration at Ellis Island for example, names are often changed by either the authorities or by the person grudgingly. Use the name you accept as a person, when you are a foreign born immigrant.

When I've emigrated from Hungary, in the early years I was called Andy and later I also accepted(grudgingly) to be called Andrew but never would fully use it. Strangers could refer me as Andrew and when they got to know me better they called me Andras, which is my real name. Andy, which I disliked back then, I just ignored when called. As ignorant as I was on spiritual matters back them, I already had a divine insight that I should not let strangers change my name just because I've left the place of my birth. Remember, how others enunciate your name is irrelevant to Numerology.

Use the commons sense. If your family, relatives and close friends call you with a certain name used in your culture, use that, always. It is insensitive to call a foreigner something else unless that person introduces himself as such. Of course, that does not stop some people who are too lazy to even try to pronounce something different. *11*

What does the Expression number reveal? It speaks volumes of your individual talents, traits. It tells you who you are. While the Life Path number tells you about your journey, the Expression number reveals your tools that endow you to cope with this journey. This number shows what characteristic you possess that make the journey a pleasant one. Usually,

---

[10] Vedic Numerologist usually use the Chaldean table but some of them creates unique tables to use.

[11] Unpronounceable names are of course a different matter but that could be a subject of a different book on geopolitics and mass migration that is happening in Europe.

and this is an esoteric idea; we are more of less well equipped to the journey at hand. This is hard for some people to believe but it is so. Remember, nothing is carved in stone rather it is written in sand. Of course some people have a mountain to climb and some have a journey that is less strenuous. This number also reveals you inner goal, your potential.

Original Sacred Alphabet
Numerical Values with Letters Assigned

1	2	3	4	5	6	7	8
(A) aleph	(B) beth	(C) chaf	(D) daleth	(E) Not Original	(U) vau	(O) ayin	(F) Not Original
(I) yod	(K) kaph	(G) gimel	(M) mem	(H) he	(V) vau	(Z) zain	(P) pe
(J) Not Original	(R) resh	(L) lamed	(T) teth	(N) nun	(W) Not Original		
(Q) qoph		(S) semakh		(X) tzaddi			
(Y) yod							

This is the table typically used for Chaldean Expression Number. Notice, that there is no nine (9).

To calculate the Expression for our example George Harrison, we must do the following;
Use the table above to calculate the vowels and consonants by marking them with a different color. There is no distinction in this exercise but later you will have calculations where either the consonants or the vowels are used. Sometimes, it is hard to figure out which is which and this allow us to gain some experience by early exposure;
Here we use the system where first and last name pertain to a given and a family name.

George	Harold	Harrison
357235	512734	51221375

25=7   22=4   26=8

As you can see the final result of George Harrison's Expression is a One(1) derived from 19 (1+9=10=1).

You can of course add all the numbers together at once which would make you a 73=10=1.

I suggest you do it this way. When dealing with software or online calculators you sometimes do not even know the method. So, Harrison being a 1, can pose the question which number is the 1 derived from. In our case it is a 10 either way.

Now you lets look at Master Cheiro's Expression using his birth name ;

William	John	Warner
6133114	1755	612552

19=1   18=9   21=3

Now you can make the same calculation for yourself;

The interpretation of Expression Numbers;

The Number 1 (Expression)

You have a desire to achieve, and do not mind doing it alone. You are the archetypical Hero, adventurous and bold. Watch out for being too blunt sharing your ideas and opinion, you are not always right. Your ego can lead you ashtray and your stubbornness can alienate others. Watch out because time is not on your side, and while being alone is fine when you are young and your whole life is ahead of you with full of possibilities, when getting older you can be very alone. Accumulate good friends early and try to keep them, because later in life it is harder to make a strong human bond.

You can be self-conscious and admire status symbols, but many times you can earn and afford the symbols of wealth, deep inside you know the futility of accumulating earthly, temporal wealth.

Watch your health and diet. Swimming is a good sport for you but other exercises are also beneficial curbing your, often overzealous energy.

It is hard for you to work for others and self-employment is the best venue for you but can work as a consultant or salesman.

The Number 2 (Expression)

You are a natural coordinator in the work environment but management as career is not ideal for you, perhaps as a supervisor you'd fulfill your potential better. Your intuitive nature can understand what others are all about, while you are easy to work, cooperate with at almost any capacity. You are usually the "power behind the throne", a person who can achieve without being in the limelight. However, guard against leaning upon others too much.

You usually marry and stay married, if you chose your mate well. You as a parent have difficulty as you are not a natural disciplinarian and dislike such roles.

The Number 3 (Expression)

You are a positive thinker with outgoing, buoyant personality. You like social gathering because your friendly disposition and demure nature. Guard against over-talkativeness or being boastful. You are creative and with abstract thinking abilities with a talent for writing, your verbal skills could lead you to sales, public speaking, or law. In your personal life, watch out for jealousy and extravagance.

The Number 4 (Expression)

Archetype of a breadwinner. Reliable and practical. Weakness in selecting friends, as you are not as intuitive and perhaps at time a little gullible. Because of your down to earth nature you are perfectly suited for the building trade, in any capacity, designer, contractor, or foreman.

The Number 5 (Expression)

You are well-read in of various subjects. You are open minded and resourceful, who loves to travel, a born explorer. You should not be looking down on people with lower education than yourself, as they likely have something to offer. You must be careful of falling into negative patterns of irresponsibility or over-indulgence of vices such as alcohol, drugs or food.

The Number 6 (Expression)

You are altruistic with deep empathy towards the downtrodden in your community. You gain solace from nature. Gardening could be one of your hobbies for your entire life. Watch out for excessive pride, jealousy or being overbearing or callous.

The Number 7 (Expression)

You are seeker of the Mysteries. Philosophical in nature, you are driven to study to test or prove various theories of the metaphysical. You are driven to seek the unseen, this religion, spirituality are possible goals in life. You however must be careful of being too secretive, miserly. When facing self-doubt you must not drink as this could be a downward spiral.

The Number 8 (Expression)

This number is interesting as it is archetype of most man who wish to balance the spiritual with the materialism. The Number 8 is textbook case for this. The number 8 symbolizes the higher and lower plane with the small upper circle and the lower, bigger circle. When the balance is struck between these two realms you will feel that you life's purpose is revealed but the paramount ingredient for this is self-mastery. This is not easy and you will not achieve this without some struggle. Seeking only wealth will always be a temptation (as 8 vibrates money), but without being well grounded and emotionally balanced, it would be fruitless pursuit. The ancient saying is applicable; "life is a bridge to cross, not to build a house on."

Watch out for misspent energy, and understand money will come naturally when you do not care about it anymore.

The Number 9 (Expression)

You are tolerant and compassionate. You are altruistic Universalist with deep empathy towards the downtrodden of the World. You strive on providing service to others but must not get too personal as your emotions would cause inner turmoil and you would lose effectiveness. Remember, that even the Biblical Jeshua said that there will always be poor[12] and unfortunate. You cannot help everybody.

---

[12] "You will always have the poor among you, but you will not always have me" Matthew 26:11

The Heart's Desire Number (Vowels of the Name)

Also called Soul Urge by some experts this number denotes the inner you. It reveals your hopes, dreams, your spirituality and motivation. Knowing this number is important because subconsciously you might be repressing this desire which is not a wholesome condition.

The Heart's Desire is calculated using only the Vowels[13] from your name. Of course now we are getting into phonetics and often determining if certain letters are Vowels or Consonants is not easy. The two odd letters are Y and W.

The letter is a vowel if there is NO restriction of the vocal cord at speech. I, E, A, O and U are vowels.

For vowels, part of the tongue moves closer to the roof of the mouth, but there is still enough of a gap.

The letter Y stands for the consonant in the word 'yoke', the vowel in the word 'myth', the vowel in the word 'funny', and the diphthong[14] in the word my. According to Decoz, The "Y" is always a consonant[15] when it is next to a vowel.

W always represents a consonant except in combination with a vowel letter, as in 'growth', 'raw', and 'how', and in a few loanwords from Welsh, like 'crwth' or 'cwm'. In some other languages, such as Finnish, y only represents a vowel sound. You must do a little research[16] and determine this for yourself. This workbook could not cover this for all languages or scenarios.

Interestingly, my name, a foreign name has a Y at the end. Nagy. Actually to make this more complicated, in Hungarian the 'gy' is one letter, pronounced like dy, or the d in 'adulation'. So I do not even concern myself with the Y and can use dy and both are part of the same syllable. Would indicate that it is perhaps a consonant, in my case. Nobody pronounces my name as in Hungarian[17], and since I have *accepted this and have lived with this for decades,* I'd use the Y as a vowel, as pronounced. So in my case;

---

[13] A, E, I, O, and U.

[14] a sound formed by the combination of two vowels in a single syllable, in which the sound begins as one vowel and moves toward another (as in *coin, loua,* and *side*).

[15] Z, B, T, G, and H and the rest of the alphabet.

[16] the Internet is a great resource for this

[17] most (not all) people pronounce my name as if I was a constant nag.

Vowels	1 1	1 7	1 1
Name	Andras	Miklos	Nagy
Consonants	542 3	4 23 3	5 3

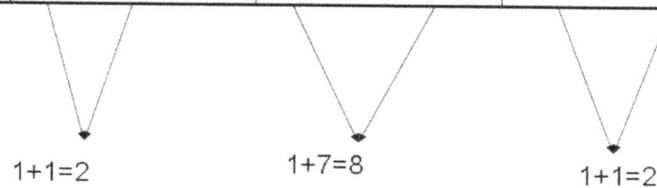

```
       1+1=2        1+7=8        1+1=2
```

My Hearts Desire is apparently 12 (1+2)=**3**

Now, lets look at George Harrison's Heart's Desire;

Vowels	57 5	1 7	1 1 7
Name	George	Harold	Harrison
Consonants	3 23	5 2 34	5 22 3 5

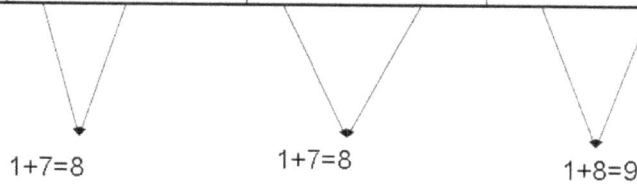

```
       1+7=8        1+7=8        1+8=9
```

George Harrison's Heart's Desire is a 8+8+9=25=**7**

Even thou the digital root is used in the ultimate analysis we always look at the numbers comprising the total. Notice, the 8's (the money number) in George Harrison's Heart's Desire? The 8 does not mean greed, rather it signifies good financial sense, and if successful; keeping what one has. Ultimately, a Mystic Beatle had the Sacred 7 as his soul desire when using the Chaldean Numerology. Using other systems you'd come up with a different and in my opinion, erroneous number.

Interpretations of the Heart's Desire Number

The Number 1 (Heart's Desire)

You have a inner urge to be original, it might not work all the time but persistence is the key. Eventually you will find your own voice or brushstroke.

You strive to be honest and loyal in your business and personal affairs.

You desire is to be heard, you need a soapbox. You have a need to be appreciated but you do not mind controversy.

You dislike monotony and the daily grind , or anything that is perceived to limit your freedom and independence.

The Number 2 (Heart's Desire)

You desire partnership, business and domestic. Being understood is important so you look for a soul mate but settle for less, beware! Often patience pays.

The Number 3 (Heart's Desire)

You desire self-expression through story telling, public speaking and writing. You endeavor to be friendly, outgoing, daring and intuitive. You crave harmony and serenity. You like children, some of you love pets. Working in the nature with wild animals is favored.

The Number 4 (Heart's Desire)

You strive for order and like the regular routine of life both domestic and work. You want clear specifications or directions in the workplace and dislike ambiguity.

The Number 5 (Heart's Desire)

Your element is a diverse and adventuresome career and desire personal freedom even when married. This could lead to problems. You are inclined to be well read and intellectual with curiosity just about everything.

The Number 6 (Heart's Desire)

You need domestic and career responsibility. You view yourself as savior whose rule extends to while mankind not only your community. You could become a globalist activist for a myriad of causes. You desire to work in a group or a choir as you strive to have a good speaking or singing voice.

The Number 7 (Heart's Desire)

You crave wisdom and you are intellectual, dislike manual labor. You are the seeker of the mysteries and aspirant of the secret schools of the esoteric. Perfection is your goal. You cherish your privacy but you'd ultimately need people.

The Number 8 (Heart's Desire)

You think big - big projects, big reward and fame, dislike being idle. Your secret desire is to be someone important either in private or government sector.

This is the conclusion of the Heart's Desire Number which essentially your desired image of yourself. Next, we shall talk about the Personality Number , which is how others really perceive you. Often you are not aware of this attribute because, you image of yourself (The Heart's Desire) and the true image you project to the outside world differ greatly.

You can do the calculation and fill out the form below of your Hearts Desire. You can verify the result by using the internet where free Numerology calculators are abundant.

Vowels			
Name			
Consonants			

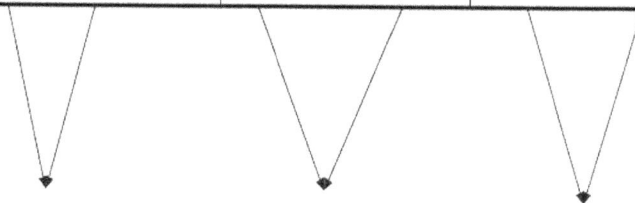

The Personality Number (Consonants of the Name)

Some Numerologists also called it Quiet Self, Inner Self which is misleading in my opinion, because what this number is fundamentally about how others see you.

Vowels	57 5	1 7	1 1 7
Name	George	Harold	Harrison
Consonants	3 23	5 2 34	5 22 3 5

$$1+7=8 \qquad 1+7=8 \qquad 1+8=9$$

By adding up the **consonants** 8+14+16=38=11 we derive a 2.

Now let us look at Master Cheiro's Personality Number;

Vowels	1 11	7	1 5
Name	William	John	Warner
Consonants	6 33	1 55	6 25 2

$$6+6=12=3 \qquad 1+10=11=2 \qquad 6+9=15=6$$

By adding up the consonants in Cheiro's name we conclude that (3+2+6=11=**2**) he is of a **Personality of Number 2**. The commonality of George and Cheiro will become obvious when you read the description of such a number. Both had a guru whom their followed conscientiously. George Harrison became a vegetarian in the late 1960s, and a devotee of the Indian mystic Paramahansa Yogananda, a guru who proselytised Kriya yoga, after he was given Yogananda's Autobiography of a Yogi by Ravi Shankar.

The Number 1 (Personality Number)

Your personality has an inner urge to be unique. This is often by projecting an unorthodox world view.

The Number 2 (Personality Number)

You desire understanding and acceptance from others. This is the reason you are sensitive of criticism and how other perceive you. You are not a leader but a follower and like it that way, but you are good judge of leadership and desire a benevolent and wise person to follow. Very often people with a number 2 posses physic abilities, other seek career in art or music.

The Number 3 (Personality Number)

You strive to be creative. You are self-conscious of your weight and look, you are a smart dresser.

The Number 4 (Personality Number)

You strive to be creative. You are self-conscious of your weight and look, you are a smart dresser.

The Number 5 (Personality Number)

You dream to be free to travel unhindered, discover new places and live for the adventure of the road.

The Number 6 (Personality Number)

Your desire to have a loving family with a beautiful home where you are surrounded with friends who admire you for who you are.

The Number 7 (Personality Number)

You pine for solitude where you are surrounded by books and a shrine where you can meditate and seek inner knowledge of mysticism. You desire a few like-minded disciples who seek your guidance in the discovery of the Ancient Wisdom. Alternatively you could be drawn into a Priesthood or other clergy depending on your family and own inclination.

The Number 8 (Personality Number)

Your main desire to be in business and make a lot of money. You think big and tell yourself that you can be a better person if you have the means to help others. Do not forget this when your boat finally arrived.

The Number 9 (Personality Number)

You dream of helping others. People feel this and you are the solace to others. You have artistic ambition and use it to further your aim.

More on the Name

When conducting a complete analysis of the personality using numerology we would have to do the work twice. Once for the full name as it is on the birth certificate, once that is completed, we must repeat the whole process for the short name. The short name is how you formally introduce yourself, or casually sign your name. Do not use middle initials, even if you sign your name that way. There is a subtle difference in the formal and casual result which can reveal some minutia of your chart.

The reason we do this is because a significant karmic debt number, missing in the full name may show up prominently in the short name. If a name change takes place later in life through marriage or for professional reasons, it could reveal or hide certain facets of character. It can also focus and intensify existing characteristics or skills that may be latent.

Numerology Workbook using Chaldean Mysticism

I would refrain from using both, short and long names in the beginning-that you can be familiar with the whole process and fully understand the numbers, without the added complexity.

Inclusion

This an important facet of Numerology. Certain letters are underrepresented or over-represented in your full name. It is possible that certain letters are omitted altogether. Inclusion is analyzing this pattern and draws important conclusions mainly how you direct your life, uphold your inner bliss by using or wasting your abilities.

George	Harold	Harrison
357235	512734	51221375

To do this you must count the letters of which the digital root is the same;

Letters having numerical value of 1: 3
Letters having numerical value of 2: 4
Letters having numerical value of 3: 4
Letters having numerical value of 4: 1
Letters having numerical value of 5: 4
Letters having numerical value of 6: 0
Letters having numerical value of 7: 3
Letters having numerical value of 8: 0

NOTE: Since we are using the Chaldean table 9 numerical value is not possible.

57

Now you can fill the blanks in the form below;

Name			
Numerical value			

Letters having numerical value of 1: _
Letters having numerical value of 2: _
Letters having numerical value of 3: _
Letters having numerical value of 4: _
Letters having numerical value of 5: _
Letters having numerical value of 6: _
Letters having numerical value of 7: _
Letters having numerical value of 8: _

To make this a more presentable, on constructing the chart we could use the following format;

Number Placement

1's	2's	3's
4's	5's	6's
7's	8's	9's

George's Chart

3	4	4
1	4	0
3	0	

Fill in the chart for your name, if the number is missing place a zero there.

Your Chart

Analyzing the inclusion.

There is no definition on what high or low representation of a letter is because some names are longer and some a very short. On average a letter is represented 2-3 times. If a letter is there more than 3 or 4 then we can assume an over-representation, if the occurrence is 0-1 then it is under represented. Use your common sense and always factor in the length of the name.

Inclusion interpretations

1 Inclusion

Average: Self-confidence, aggressive, pride, originality, determination, and will-power.
Too many: Ability to finish what is started, determined and courageous, assertive, focused.
Few or none: Selfless, easy going, interested in others, lacks drive and confidence.

2 Inclusion

Average: Social, friendly, well-behaved, cooperative
Too many: A mediator, romantic, sensitive, sometimes timid, patient with others
Few or none: inconsiderate, boorish, inflexible.

3 Inclusion

Average: Creative with childlike imagination, expressive orally and in writing, happy and sociable.
Too many: Impatient, boastful, talkative, talented, will persevere if inspired but dislikes physical labor.
Few or none: Has issues with self-image and self-expression, shy and withdrawn.

4 Inclusion

Average: Focus and correct application of self gives ability to accomplish task with objective and orderly manner.
Too many: Good at focusing but bogged down with details, can be stubborn and narrow minded.
Few or none: Dislikes work and routine tasks, impatient and needs assistance.

5 Inclusion

Average: flexible to changing circumstances, welcomes adventure and variety, uses personal freedom in a measured, matured way.
Too many: Scattered, restless, fails to finish tasks by losing interest early. Can become overindulgent in the pleasures of the flesh.
Few or none: set in his way, dislikes crowds and lacks interest in life.

6 Inclusion

Average: Humane, dutiful , very domestically inclined, more luxurious the better, adjust well to most situations, very aware of right and wrong.

Too many: Generous, responsible, can be entrenched in tradition and has fanatical tendencies. Can become heartbroken if expectations are not met.

Few or none: Has hard time accepting responsibility, and has difficulty seeing things for what they are. Could be overbearing at home.

7 Inclusion

Average: Sharp, analytical mind, full of empathy and compassion. Discriminating with observation and precision with talent to seek the unknown.

Too many: A genius - this person is hard to know well because of secretiveness and very selective of whom he shares his thoughts.

Few or none: More open and outdoing than the average 7. Open minded and balanced, they find inner peace and happiness.

8 Inclusion

Average: Appreciates the material benefits of hard work. Self-efficient and entrepreneurial, reliable in crisis situations.

Too many: A manager and organizer of others. Could be overly materialistic, a miser, but often a very good at evaluating others and working in the community.

Few or none: Lacks the ability to handle money responsively. Not motivated by money, and often needs to fall back to the charity of others.

Part III. Advanced Numerology

The Maturity Number

This is very important number which comes to light at the end of your formative years, the exact time varies from person to person, usually between age thirty and thirty five. This number is the real, mature you with one underlying theme.

The Maturity Number is constructed by adding the Life Path to the Expression (basically a combination of vibrations from the birth-date and name)

This number is the greatest cue to your being and understanding precisely what it vibrates would make your life more meaningful.

Life Path digit		
Expression digit		
Total +		= Maturity

The Number 1 (Maturity Number)

Shed your childhood dependence. Avoid procrastination. You can become a good leader, manager if you apply hard work and diligence. It is time to embark on adventures and become your own man. If you have multiple 1's in your chart, especially among your core numbers; you'd be wise to be guarded against becoming pig-headed and bossy.

The Number 2 (Maturity Number)

Seek counsel and advice at the right place. Avoid bad company but trust your instinct when you encounter people . You can become a good artist, or even a spiritual healer if you find your center and the right environment. It is time to seek harmony and inner peace in philosophy or religion. Guard against tendencies that could lead towards inferiority complex.

The Number 3 (Maturity Number)

As you grow older you'd find yourself more and more extroverted and outgoing. You will master verbal communications and could become an excellent public speaker. Your clothing and style will match your expressive exuberance. Guard against self-importance and scattering your talents in too many directions.

The Number 4 (Maturity Number)

When your maturity arrives you will complete your methodology to organize yourself and materialize concepts and ideas. You are practical and down-to-earth. Others could also benefit from you as you are dependable and helpful towards family and friends. Be careful not to become too set in your ways and remain open-minded.

The Number 5 (Maturity Number)

Nothing can stop you now. Your personal power will manifest as you become better rounded and resourceful. You will take up any opportunity to travel and experience other lands and culture.

The Number 6 (Maturity Number)

As you grow older, you would become more caring of the well-being of your family and community. Your need to correct the ills of the world would draw you into professions such as a doctor, nurse, or therapist.

The Number 7 (Maturity Number)

As you mature, you would become more interested in the greater questions in life. Your keen intellect will lead you towards Philosophy, metaphysics or religion. Your inner guide will be louder and you will be inclined to listen, which is usually a beneficial thing to do. If you have other 7's in your chart you should guard against becoming a hermit and alienated from society. However if you have no other 7's in your core chart, then you could easily become focused on your solitary pursuit and easily could become expert in your field of study.

The Number 8 (Maturity Number)

As you leave you formative years, success and monetary reward will be close at hand. As you'd become more knowledgeable, you commitment towards you career will be stronger. You must be careful that the monetary goal should not be the only drive towards success or you entering a dangerous realm of money worship and that can lead towards self-destruction.

Having more 8's in your core numbers would indicate this danger, described above. Even so you can be self aware and make the necessary corrections. If you core numbers have no or only a few 8's, this could make your striving towards financial independence come to fruition easier.

The Number 9 (Maturity Number)

Your concern towards mankind's well being is becoming stronger as you mature. This motivation could lead you towards public service or activism. You are not satisfied with your immediate community but you are concerned about the whole world, thus you might seek opportunities in very poor, undeveloped places in the world. If you have several 9's in your core numbers, then you must be careful of becoming overly zealous or fanatical. However if you have zero or just a few 9's then it will make your life more grounded and satisfying.

Forecasting in Numerology

You can find any future (or past) date for a given year by adding the month and the day of your birthday, plus the Universal Year number for the date in question. The result is called the Personal Year. For example someone born on December 21ˢᵗ (12+21=33=**6**) wants to find the future year (2017), which is the Universal Year (2017). 2017=10=**1**. So the Personal Year for 2017 is =6+1=**7**.

Let us examine this a bit more in detail; The **Personal Year** is derived from your individual birth date and tells you more specifically *what Cosmic and inner influences you'll personally be resolving during the year.* The **Universal Year** *is for all men on the Planet, Cosmic forces equally felt by everybody* and is calculated by adding the numbers of the current year together.

Double-digit Numbers

As Numbers through 1-9 are pertaining to the physical plane the double-digit numbers have more occult connotation. For a personal analysis we use the single digits but for other venue and the deeper understanding Numerology we must study and understand these compound numbers.

Number 10

Symbolized as the "Wheel of Fortune". It is a number of honor, of faith and self-confidence, of rise and fall; one's name will be known for good or evil, according to one's desires; it is a fortunate number in the sense that one's plans are likely to be carried out.

Number 11

This is an ominous number to occultists. It gives warning of hidden dangers, trial, and treachery from others. It has a symbol of a "Clenched Hand", and "a Lion Muzzled", and of a person who will have great difficulties to contend against.

Number 12

This symbolizes sacrifice and victim-hood. It warns of a danger what others have planned either to harm or for idle amusement.

Number 13

Contrary to the popular belief this is not an unlucky number. It is complicated to understand but ancient writings state that whomever understand this number will be given great powers. The number symbolizes change of plans and locales, it represents power but if it used improperly it can destroy the beholder. The pictorial representation is the skeleton and perhaps this is why it always had a misunderstanding from the neophytes. It warns of the unknown and unaccepted.

Number 14

This is a number of movement, combination of people and things, and danger from natural forces such as storm, water, air or fire. This number is fortunate for dealings with money, speculation and changes in business, but there is always a strong element of risk and danger attached to it, but generally owing to the actions and recklessness of others. If this number comes out in calculations of future events the person should be warned to act with caution and prudence.

Number 15

This is a number of occult significance, of magic and mystery; but as a rule it does not represent the higher side of occultism, its meaning being that the persons represented by it will use every art of magic they can to carry out their purpose. If associated with a good or fortunate single number, it can be very lucky and powerful, but if associated with one of the peculiar numbers, such as a 4 or an 8, the person it represents will not hesitate to use any sort of art, or even "black-magic," to gain what he or she desires.

It is peculiarly associated with "good talkers," often with eloquence, gifts of music and art and a dramatic personality, combined with a certain voluptuous temperament and strong personal magnetism. For obtaining money, gifts, and favors from others it is a fortunate number.

Number 16

This number has a most peculiar occult symbolism. It is pictured by "a Tower Struck by Lightning from which a man is falling with a Crown on his head." It is also called "the Shattered Citadel".

It gives warning of some strange fatality awaiting one, also danger of accidents and defeat of one's plans. If it appears as a "compound" number relating to the future, it is a warning sign that should be carefully noted and plans made in advance in the endeavor to avert its fatalistic tendency.

Number 17

This is a highly spiritual number, and is expressed in symbolism by the 8-pointed Sta r of Venus; a symbol of "Peace and love". It is also called "the Star of the Magi" and expresses that the person it represents has risen superior in spirit to the trials and difficulties of his life or his career . It is considered a "Number of immortality" and that the person's name "lives after him". It is a fortunate number if it works out in relation to future events, provided it is not associated with the single number of fours and eights.

Number 18

This number has a difficult symbolism to translate. It is pictured as "a rayed moon from which drops of blood are falling; a wolf and a hungry dog are seen below catching the falling drops of blood in their opened mouths, while still lower a crab is seen hastening to join them." It is symbolic of materialism striving to destroy the spiritual side of the nature. It generally associates a person with bitter quarrels, even family ones, also with war, social upheavals, revolutions; and in some cases it indicates making money and position thorough wars or by wars. It is however a warning of treachery, deception by others, also danger from the elements such as storms, danger from water, fires and explosions. When this "compound" number appears in working out dates in advance, such a date should be taken with a great amount of care, caution and circumspection.

Number 19

This number is regarded as fortunate and extremely favorable. It is symbolized as "the Sun" and is called "the Prince of Heaven." It is a number promising happiness, success, esteem and honor and promises success in one's plan for the future.

Number 20

This number is called "the Awakening"; also "the Judgment". It is symbolized by the figure of a winged angel sounding a trumpet, while from below a man, a woman, and a child are seen rising from a tomb with their hands clasped in prayer. This number has a peculiar interpretation; the call to action, but for some great purpose, cause or duty. It is not a material number and consequently is a doubtful one as far as worldly success is concerned. If used in relation to a future event, it denotes delays, hindrances to one's plans, which can only be conquered through the development of the spiritual side of nature.

Number 21

This number is symbolized by the picture of "the Universe", and it is also called "the Crown of the Magi". It is a number of advancement, honors, elevation in life and general success. It means victory after long initiation and tests of determination. It is a fortunate number of promise if it appears in any connection with future events.

Number 22

This number is symbolized by a " a Good Man blinded by the folly of others, with a knapsack on his back full of Arrows". In this picture he appears to offer no defense against a ferocious tiger which is attacking him. It is a warning number of illusion and delusion, a good person who lives in a fool's paradise; a dreamer of dreams who awakens only when surrounded by danger. It is also a number of false judgment owing to the influence of others. As a number in connection with future events, it is a warning and its meaning should be carefully noted.

Number 23

This number is called "the Royal Star of the Lion." It is a promise of success, help from superiors and protection from those in high places. In dealing with future events it is a most fortunate number and a promise of success of one's plan's.

Number 24

This number is also fortunate; it promises the assistance and association of those of rank and position with one's plans; it also denotes gain through love and the opposite sex; it is a favorable number when it comes out in relation to future events.

Number 25

This is a number denoting strength gained through experience, and benefits obtained through observation of people and things. It is not deemed exactly "lucky", as its success is given through strife and trials in an earlier life. It is favorable when it appears in regard to the future.

Number 26

This number is full of the gravest warnings for the future. It foreshadows disasters brought about by association with others; ruin by bad speculations, by partnerships, unions and bad advice. If it comes out in connection with future events one should carefully consider the path one is treading.

Number 27

This is a good number and is symbolized as "the Scepter.[18]" It is a promise of authority, power and command. It indicates that reward will come from the productive intellect; that the creative faculties have sown good seeds that will reap a harvest. Persons with this "command" number at their back should carry out their own ideas and plans. It is a fortunate number if it appears in any connection with future events.

Number 28

This number is full of contradictions. It indicates a person of great promise and possibilities who is likely to see all taken away from him unless he carefully provides for the future. It indicates loss through trust in others, opposition and competition in trade, danger of loss through law, and the likelihood of having to begin life's road over and over again.

Number 29

It is not a fortunate number for the indication of future events. This number indicates uncertainties, treachery, and deception of others; it foreshadows trials, tribulation, and unexpected dangers, unreliable friends, and grief and deception caused by members of the opposite sex. It gives grave warning if it comes out in anything concerning future events.

Number 30

This is a number of thoughtful deduction, retrospection, and mental superiority over one's fellows, but as it seems to belong completely to the mental plane, the persons it represents, are likely to put all material things on one side — not because they have to, but because they wish to do so. For this reason it is neither fortunate nor unfortunate, for either depends on the mental outlook of the person it represents. It can be all powerful, but it is just as often indifferent according to the will or desire of the person.

---

[18] A scepter is a symbolic ornamental staff or wand held in the hand by a ruling monarch as an item of royal or imperial insignia.

Number 31

This number is very similar to the preceding one, except that the person it represents is even more self-contacted, lonely, and isolated from his fellows. It is not a fortunate number from a worldly or material standpoint.

Number 32

This number has a magical power like the single 5, or the "command" numbers 14 and 23. It is usually associated with combinations of people or nations. It is a fortunate number if the person it represents holds to his own judgment and opinions; if not, his plans are likely to be wrecked by the stubbornness and stupidity of others. It is a favorable number if it appears in connection with future events.

Number 33

This number has no potency of its own and consequently has the same meaning as 24, which is also a 6.

Number 34

This number has no potency of its own and consequently has the same meaning as 25, which is also a 7.

Number 35

This number has no potency of its own and consequently has the same meaning as 26, which is also a 8.

Number 36

This number has no potency of its own and consequently has the same meaning as 27, which is also a 9.

Number 37

This number has a distinct potency of its own. It is a number of good and fortunate friendships in love, and in combinations connected with the opposite sex. It is also good for partnerships of all kinds. It is a fortunate indication if it appears in connection with future events.

Number 38

Has the same meaning as the number 29.

Number 39

Has the same meaning as the number 30.

Number 40

Has the same meaning as the number 31.

Number 41

Has the same meaning as the number 32.

Number 42

Has the same meaning as the number 24.

Number 43

This is an unfortunate number. It is symbolized by the signs of revolution, upheaval, strife, failure, and prevention and is not a fortunate number if it comes out in calculation relating to future events.

Number 44

Has the same meaning as the number 26.

Number 45

Has the same meaning as the number 27.

Number 46

Has the same meaning as the number 37.

Number 47

Has the same meaning as the number 29.

Number 48

Has the same meaning as the number 30.

Number 49

Has the same meaning as the number 31.

Number 50

Has the same meaning as the number 32.

Number 51

This number has a very powerful potency of its own. It represents the nature of the warrior; it promises sudden advancement in whatever one undertakes; it is especially favorable for those in military or naval life and for leaders in any cause. At the same time it threatens enemies, dangers and the likelihood of assassination.

Number 52

Has the same meaning as the number 43.

Part IV. Mysticism and Numbers

Karma and Reincarnation

Karmic Debt numbers are 13, 14, 16, and 19. These double-digit numbers take on great significance when they are found in the Life Path, Expression, Heart's Desire, Personality.

Karmic Debt indicates some carried over burden from our past lives.

For example:

William	John	Warner
6133114	1755	612552

19=1 19 is a Karmic Debt Number

18=9

21=3

Master Cheiro's (William John Walker) first name has a Karmic debt of 19, which is significant when we look back of his controversy of missing funds, consequently losing his gift and going to prison. This number indicates misuse of power, and paying back something taken.

It is interesting to note that we often face the same karmic challenge again and again, almost as if the Universe wanting to test us again for past transgressions. Pride and Ego can trap us into this revolving door of birth death cycle, repeating the same mistakes, again and again unless we learn to love and cooperate with one and other.

When the Karmic Debt number is found as the

- Expression number you will feel its effect on a more continuous, but less dramatic, basis, affecting mostly your working life.
- Heart's Desire number you will have a inclination to make bad decisions in your lifestyle, including relationships with the opposite sex and friends.
- Personality number; its influence will be mostly felt in social interaction. This can be anything from simply making bad impressions to silly remarks, bad taste in clothing, Issues with Health can also be impacted.
- Maturity number; it is usually strong during your late formative years as well as the later part of your productive years (late forties and early fifties).
- Life Path Number; it is felt on occasions throughout your life but not as a constant burden. With vigilance this Karmic Debt can be resolved.

Number 13 (Karmic Debt)

This karmic number has to do with effort. It is apparent that you were a bit lazy[19] in a past life, thus not fulfilling your potential and given abilities. When you have this number it is paramount to finish what you have started, and lots of patience because you will be tested.

Number 14 (Karmic Debt)

This karmic number has to do with abusing freedom. It could be your own or others. in a past life, thus in this time around there is a debt to be paid. When you have this number be warned that you life will not be smooth and orderly. Keep away from addictive activities or substances as they can enslave you.

Number 16 (Karmic Debt)

This karmic number is very powerful. It can also be very rewarding as it is the destruction of the old and rebuilding in its place something better. When you have this number you would feel the urge to reinvent yourself by abandoning old habits and lifestyle.

Number 19 (Karmic Debt)

This karmic number is about personal power. You will be put in situations where you will have to rely on your own resources and wit. Expect some turmoil and surprises in your life with this number in your shadow. At times you would feel alone and abandoned, but do not

---

[19]Especially, when found in Expression Number

be afraid. Most situations can be resolved when your doubts and fear subsides and your inner strength resurfaces.

The other karmic number is a Karmic Lesson and we shall explain it in detail under the Part II. of this book.

What is Karma?

Karma is not a punishment nor it is a result of a vengeful God. It is simply the result of your actions, thoughts in this or a past life. This is your individual Karma. There is a group Karma and even Nations carry certain Karmic past. All this is Natures Law of that states all actions will have a reaction. Karma and Reincarnation go hand in hand. Some people believe in one and not the other, and some people reject the whole idea. For me it was logical to accept the whole package, as life's seemingly cruel and unexplained twists and turns, all of the sudden started making sense. The question; "how a merciful God can allow this?" now had at least an answer. Not an easy explanation but at least a plausible one. My former teacher wrote a very good book on Karma and I wholeheartedly recommend it if you wish to learn more about this subject.

Reincarnation

This idea, along with the Law of Karma, is found in many religions. It is said that even the Bible had certain references of Karma/Reincarnation, some remained in place, while some were removed on purpose. The Hindu doctrine of Reincarnation maintains that the spirit is everlasting while the soul contains imprints that pertain to each and every incarnation. We return to correct mistakes made in past lives. Recently there have been serious studies of children who had past life memories to the astonishing detail, some had names and places mentioned that they could have never known unless their past lives experience were true and factual.

More about Numbers

"The laws of nature are but the mathematical thoughts of God." — Euclid

In this chapter we examine the Numbers according to the Ancient Wisdom.

Calculating the Numerical representation of a WORD, Ideally The first step in obtaining the correct value of a word is to resolve it back into its original tongue.[20] Only words of Greek or Hebrew derivation can be successfully analyzed by this method, and *all words must be spelled in their most ancient and complete forms.* Ideally, Old Testament words and names, therefore, must be translated back into the early Hebrew characters and New Testament words into the Greek. Gematria will help to clarify this principle.

Gematria

The *gematria* is an Assyro-Babylonian system of numerology later adopted into Jewish culture in unique in that it assigns numerical value to a word or phrase in the belief that words or phrases with identical numerical values bear some relation to each other. Derived from this philosophy each letter of the Hebrew alphabet has a distinct Numerical value. So according to the Hebrew mysticism the Kabala, it states that God's is English name *Jehovah*, is inadequate, so when seeking the numerical value of the name *Jehovah* it is necessary to resolve the name into its Hebrew letters. It becomes יהוה, and is read from right to left. The Hebrew letters are: ה, He; ו, Vau; ה, He; י, Yod; and when reversed into the English order from left to right read: *Yod-He-Vau-He. Yod* equals 10. *He* equals 5, *Vau* equals 6, and the second *He* equals 5. Therefore, 10+5+6+5=26, a synonym of *Jehovah*. If the English letters were used, the answer obviously would not be correct.

The Number 1 (Monad)

THE Monad has been defined by the ancients as the principal and element of numbers, which while multitude can be lessened by subtraction, is itself deprived of every number and remains stable and firm"; hence as number it is indivisible, it remains immutable, and even

---

[20] this is why I favor the Chaldean or as some say phonetic system.

multiplied into itself remains itself only, since once one is still one, and the monad multiplied by the monad remains the immutable monad to infinity. It remains by itself among numbers, for no number can be taken from it, or separated from its unity.

The Number 2 (Dyad or Duad)

As was the case with the Monad so the Duad also was said to represent a large number of different objects and ideas; things indeed so dissimilar that it is difficult to understand how such multiplicity of opinion arose.

In his book, *Numbers*, W. Wynn Westcott says of the duad: "it was called 'Audacity,' from its being the earliest number to separate itself from the Divine One; from the 'Adytum of God-nourished Silence,' as the Chaldean oracles say."

And first it is the general opposite to the Monad, the cause of dissimilitude, the interval between the Infinite of Numbers and the Monad. Of figures, those which are characterized by equality and sameness have relation to the Monad; but those in which inequality and difference predominate are allied to the Dyad.

The Number 3 (Triad)

THE NUMBER 3 OR TRIAD - The Ancients had observed that the Triad is the first odd number, also is the first perfect number.

The Pythagoreans related it to Physiology; showing that they fully understood the three layers of human existence. Physical, Mental and Emotional.

The Druids also paid a special attention to this number; and even their poems are noted as being composed in Triads. It is not necessary here to enlarge upon the transcendent importance of the Christian Trinity. In old paintings we often see a Trinity of Jesus with John and Mary. More importantly this number also signifies the trinity of Guide, Guru and Master of the Ancient Wisdom.

Among the Brahmins there were three great Vedas; three Margas or ways of salvation; three Gunas, the Satva, quiescence; Rajas, desire; and Tamas, decay. Three Lokas, Swarga, Bhumi and Patala; heaven, earth and hell. Three Jewels of wisdom, the Tri-ratnas; Buddha, Dharma and Sanga. The three Fires being the three aspects of the human soul, Atma, Buddhi and Manas. There were three prongs of the trident, and three eyes in the forehead of Siva. Note also the 3-syllabled Holy Word AUM.

It is the first equilibrium of unities; therefore, Pythagoras said that Apollo gave oracles from a tripod, and advised offer of libation three times. The keywords to the qualities of the triad are friendship, peace, justice, prudence, piety, temperance, and virtue. The following deities partake of the principles of the triad: Saturn (ruler of time), Latona, Cornucopiæ, Ophion (the great serpent), Thetis, Hecate, Polyhymnia (a Muse), Pluto, Triton, President of the Sea, Tritogenia, Achelous, and the Faces, Furies, and Graces. This number is called wisdom, because men organize the present, foresee the future, and benefit by the experiences of the fast. It is cause of wisdom and understanding. The triad is the number of knowledge--music, geometry, and astronomy, and the science of the celestials and terrestrials. Pythagoras taught that the cube of this number had the power of the lunar circle.

The sacredness of the triad and its symbol--the triangle--is derived from the fact that it is made up of the monad and the duad. The monad is the symbol of the Divine Father and the duad of the Great Mother. The triad being made of these two is therefore androgynous and is symbolic of the fact that God gave birth to His worlds out of Himself, who in His creative aspect is always symbolized by the triangle. The monad passing into the duad was thus capable of becoming the parent of progeny, for the duad was the womb of Meru, within which the world was incubated and within which it still exists in embryo.

The Number 4 (Tetrad)

Also referred as the tetrad was esteemed by the Pythagoreans as the primogenial number, the root of all things, the fountain of Nature and the most perfect number. All tetrads are intellectual; they have an emergent order and encircle the world as the Empyreum passes through it. Why the Pythagoreans expressed God as a tetrad is explained in a sacred discourse ascribed to Pythagoras, wherein God is called the Number of Numbers. This is because the decad, or 10, is composed of 1, 2, 3, and 4. The number 4 is symbolic of God because it is symbolic of the first four numbers. Moreover, the tetrad is the center of the week, being halfway between 1 and 7. The tetrad is also the first geometric solid.

Pythagoras maintained that the soul of man consists of a tetrad, the four powers of the soul being mind, science, opinion, and sense. The tetrad connects all beings, elements, numbers, and seasons; nor can anything be named which does not depend upon the tetractys. It is the Cause and Maker of all things, the intelligible God, Author of celestial and sensible good, Plutarch interprets this tetractys, which he said was also called the world, to be 36, consisting of the first four odd numbers added to the first four even numbers, thus:

$$1 + 3 + 5 + 7 = 16$$
$$2 + 4 + 6 + 8 = 20$$
$$36$$

Keywords given to the tetrad are impetuosity, strength, virility, two-mothered, and the key keeper of Nature, because the universal constitution cannot be without it. It is also called harmony and the first profundity. The following deities partook of the nature of the tetrad: Hercules, Mercury, Vulcan, Bacchus, and Urania (one of the Muses).

The triad represents the primary colors and the major planets, while the tetrad represents the secondary colors and the minor planets. From the first triangle come forth the seven spirits, symbolized by a triangle and a square. These together form the Masonic apron.

The Number 5 (Pentad)

The pentad is the union of an odd and an even number (3 and 2). Among the Ancients, the pentagram was a sacred symbol of light, health, and vitality. It also symbolized the fifth element--ether--because it is free from the disturbances of the four lower elements. It is called equilibrium, because it divides the perfect number 10 into two equal parts.

The pentad is symbolic of Nature, for, when multiplied by itself it returns into itself, just as grains of wheat, starting in the form of seed, pass through Nature's processes and reproduce the seed of the wheat as the ultimate form of their own growth. Other numbers multiplied by themselves produce other numbers, but only 5 and 6 multiplied by themselves represent and retain their original number as the last figure in their products.

The pentad represents all the superior and inferior beings. It is sometimes referred to as the hierophant, or the priest of the Mysteries, because of its connection with the spiritual ethers, by means of which mystic development is attained. Keywords of the pentad are reconciliation, alternation, marriage, immortality, cordiality, Providence, and sound. Among the deities who partook of the nature of the pentad were Pallas, Nemesis, Bubastia (Bast), Venus, Androgynia, Cytherea, and the messengers of Jupiter.

The tetrad (the elements) plus the monad equals the pentad. The Pythagoreans taught that the elements of earth, fire, air, and water were permeated by a substance called ether-- the basis of vitality and life. Therefore, they chose the five-pointed star, or pentagram, as the symbol of vitality, health, and interpenetration.

It was customary for the philosophers to conceal the element of earth under the symbol of a dragon, and many of the heroes of antiquity were told to go forth and slay the dragon. Hence, they drove their sword (the monad) into the body of the dragon (the tetrad). This resulted in the formation of the pentad, a symbol of the victory of the spiritual nature over the material nature. The four elements are symbolized in the early Biblical writings as the four rivers that poured out of Garden of Eden. The elements themselves are under the control of the composite Cherubim of Ezekiel.

The Number 6 (Hexad)

The Ancients, or as Clement of Alexandria conceived, the creation of the world according to both the prophets and the ancient Mysteries. It was called by the Pythagoreans the perfection of all the parts. This number was particularly sacred to Orpheus, and also to the Fate, Lachesis, and the Muse, Thalia. It was called the form of forms, the articulation of the universe, and the maker of the soul.

Among the Greeks, harmony and the soul were considered to be similar in nature, because all souls are harmonic. The hexad is also the symbol of marriage, because it is formed by the union of two triangles, one masculine and the other feminine. Among the keywords given to the hexad are: time, for it is the measure of duration; panacea, because health is equilibrium, and the hexad is a balance number; the world, because the world, like the hexad, is often seen to consist of contraries by harmony; omnisufficient[21], because its parts are sufficient for totality (3 +2 + 1 = 6); unwearied, because it contains the elements of immortality.

The Number 7 (Heptad)

Manly P. Hall[22] writes in *The Secret Teachings of All Ages* ; "The Ancients referred to the number 7 as "worthy of veneration." It was held to be the number of religion, because man is controlled by seven celestial spirits to whom it is proper for him to make offerings. It was called the number of life, because it was believed that human creatures born in the seventh month of embryonic life usually lived, but those born in the eighth month often died. One author called it the Motherless Virgin, Minerva, because it was nor born of a mother but out of the crown, or the head of the Father, the monad. Keywords of the heptad are fortune, occasion, custody, control, government, judgment, dreams, voices, sounds, and that which leads all things to their end. Deities whose attributes were expressed by the heptad were Ægis, Osiris, Mars, and Cleo (one of the Muses)."

Among many ancient nations the heptad is a sacred number. The Elohim of the Jews were supposedly seven in number. They were the Spirits of the Dawn, more commonly known as the Archangels controlling the planets. The seven Archangels, with the three spirits controlling the sun in its threefold aspect, constitute the 10, the sacred Pythagorean decad. The mysterious Pythagorean tetractys, or four rows of dots, increasing from 1 to 4, was symbolic of the stages of creation. The great Pythagorean truth that all things in Nature are

---

[21] a biblical description of God (abundant without limits)

[22] MPH was a Canadian-born author and mystic. He is best known for his 1928 work *The Secret Teachings of All Ages*.

regenerated through the decad, or 10, is subtly preserved in Freemasonry through these grips being effected by the uniting of 10 fingers, five on the hand of each person.

The 3 (spirit, mind, and soul) descend into the 4 (the world), the sum being the 7, or the mystic nature of man, consisting of a threefold spiritual body and a fourfold material form. These are symbolized by the cube, which has six surfaces and a mysterious seventh point within. The six surfaces are the directions: north, east, south, west, up, and down; or, front, back, right, left, above, and below; or again, earth, fire, air, water, spirit, and matter. In the midst of these stands the 1, which is the upright figure of man, from whose center in the cube radiate six pyramids. From this comes the great occult axiom: "The center is the father of the directions, the dimensions, and the distances."

The heptad is the number of the law, because it is the number of the Makers of Cosmic law, the Seven Spirits before the Throne.

The Number 8 (Ogdoad)

The Number 8 was sacred because it was the number of the first cube, which form had eight corners, and was the only evenly-even number under 10 (1-2-4-8-4-2-1). Thus, the 8 is divided into two 4's, each 4 is divided into two 2's, and each 2 is divided into two 1's, thereby reestablishing the monad. Among the keywords of the ogdoad are love, counsel, prudence, law, and convenience. Among the divinities partaking of its nature were Panarmonia, Rhea, Cibele, Cadmæa, Dindymene, Orcia, Neptune, Themis, and Euterpe (a Muse).

The ogdoad was a mysterious number associated with the Eleusinian Mysteries of Greece and the Cabiri. It was called the little holy number. It derived its form partly from the twisted snakes on the Caduceus of Hermes and partly from the serpentine motion of the celestial bodies; possibly also from the moon's nodes.

The Number 9 (Ennead)

The 9 was the first square of an odd number (3x3). It was associated with failure and shortcoming because it fell short of the perfect number 10 by one. It was called the called the number of man, because of the nine months of his embryonic life. Among its keywords are ocean and horizon, because to the ancients these were boundless. The ennead is the limitless number because there is nothing beyond it but the infinite 10. It was called boundary and limitation, because it gathered all numbers within itself.

The 9 was looked upon as evil, because it was an inverted 6. According to the Eleusinian Mysteries, it was the number of the spheres through which the consciousness passed on its way to birth. Because of its close resemblance to the spermatozoon, the 9 has been associated with germinal life.

The Number 10 (Decad)

The 10 according to the Ancient Wisdom, is the greatest of numbers, not only because it is the tetractys (the 10 dots) but because it comprehends all arithmetic and harmonic proportions. Pythagoras said that 10 is the nature of number, because all nations reckon to it and when they arrive at it they return to the monad. The decad was called both heaven and the world, because the former includes the latter. Being a perfect number, the decad was applied by the Pythagoreans to those things relating to age, power, faith, necessity, and the power of memory. It was also called unwearied, because, like God, it was tireless. The Pythagoreans divided the heavenly bodies into ten orders. They also stated that the decad perfected all numbers and comprehended within itself the nature of odd and even, moved and unmoved, good and ill.

The decimal system can probably be traced back to the time when it was customary to reckon on the fingers, these being among the most primitive of calculating devices and still in use among many aboriginal peoples.

What is the *tetractys?* Its image is an equilateral triangle based on the essential numbers 1 (top), 2, 3 and 4 (base), whose sum is the "perfect" number 10 ($1 + 2 + 3 + 4 = 10$).

The magic of the *tetractys*

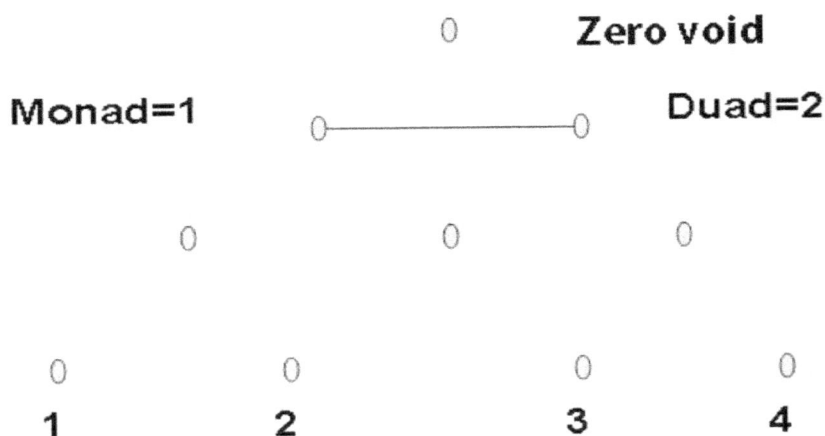

0   **Zero void**

Monad=1   0————————0   **Duad=2**

0   0   0

0   0   0   0

1   **2**   **3**   **4**

•the first row (top) represented zero dimensions (a point)
•the second row represented one dimension (a line of two points)
•the third row represented two dimensions (a plane defined by a triangle of three points)
•the fourth row represented three dimensions (a tetrahedron defined by four points)

NOTE: The first four numbers are the archetypical "creation numbers" and the ancients thought of the rest of numbers (5, 6, 7, 8, 9) as "normal" numbers, distinctly different from the first four.